# THE HOLOCAUST

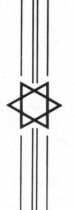

## Selected Documents in Eighteen Volumes

**John Mendelsohn**
*EDITOR*

**Donald S. Detwiler**
*ADVISORY EDITOR*

*A GARLAND SERIES*

# CONTENTS OF THE SERIES

# THE HOLOCAUST

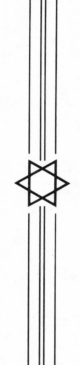

## 14. Relief and Rescue of Jews from Nazi Oppression
### 1943–1945

*Introduction by*
John Mendelsohn

GARLAND PUBLISHING, INC.
NEW YORK • LONDON
1982

Library of Congress Cataloging in Publication Data
Main entry under title:

Relief and rescue of Jews from Nazi oppression, 1943–1945.

(The Holocaust ; 14)
1. World War, 1939–1945—Jews—Rescue—Sources.
I. Mendelsohn, John, 1928–      .   II. Title.
D810.J4H655   vol. 14   940.53'15'03924s      81-80322
ISBN 0-8240-4888-1   [940.53'15'03924]      AACR2

*Design by Jonathan Billing*

The volumes in this series have been printed on acid-free,
250-year-life paper.

Printed in the United States of America

# ACKNOWLEDGMENTS

I owe a debt of gratitude to many people who aided me during various stages of preparing these eighteen volumes. Of these I would like to mention by name a few without whose generous efforts this publication would have been impossible. I would like to thank Donald B. Schewe of the Franklin D. Roosevelt Library in Hyde Park, New York, for his speedy and effective help. Sally Marcks and Richard Gould of the Diplomatic Branch of the National Archives in Washington, D.C., extended help beyond their normal archival duties, as did Timothy Mulligan and George Wagner from the Modern Military Branch. Edward J. McCarter in the Still Picture Branch helped a great deal. I would also like to thank my wife, Tish, for letting me spend my evenings during the past few years with these volumes rather than with her and our children, Michael and Lisa.

J. M.

# INTRODUCTION

Relief and rescue of Jews from Nazi persecution and oppression proceeded through many phases. The first major wave of rescue was largely based on emigration. With the coming of the "Final Solution," however, channels of emigration froze, and only a trickle remained open in the Balkans, often involving neutral countries. Much of the relief and rescue carried out in the later phases of World War II involved the work of the War Refugee Board.

The War Refugee Board evolved as a response to many pressures: more extensive knowledge of American authorities of the extent of the Nazi extermination program, cries for help from the American and foreign Jewish communities, humanitarian considerations, and the desire of the United States to take the lead in aiding the victims in order to encourage other nations to follow suit. This last pressure did not result entirely from altruistic motives; the United States was reluctant to become the only recipient of hundreds of thousands of helpless, demoralized survivors. Yet, on the whole, the administration of this country acted slowly in forming the board.

When formally established in January 1944 through an executive order, the War Refugee Board consisted of the secretaries of state, treasury, and war as policymakers. During the first year of its existence John W. Pehle, assistant secretary of the treasury, directed the board's activities; Brigadier General William O'Dwyer succeeded him and served until the dissolution of the board in the fall of 1945. The board acted through attachés for refugees, accredited with diplomatic status and posted strategically at American embassies and legations in allied countries, neutral nations, and recently conquered areas.

In order to achieve effective means of rescuing victims of Nazi oppression, the board cooperated in this endeavor not only with other governments but also with private individuals and organizations—the Jewish Agency, the American Jewish Committee, the World Jewish Congress, the American Jewish Joint Distribution Committee among them. The War Refugee Board provided money and licenses for rescue and relief and coordinated these activities. In the early phase of these operations the focus was on channeling children from southern France and the Balkans to safety. Later activities dealt with the relief of Hungarian Jews and conditions in concentration camps.

As the tragic fate of the Hungarian Jews unfolded, the War Refugee Board made a

Section of a photograph of Auschwitz-Birkenau taken by the
Mediterranean Allied Photo Reconnaissance Wing. The labels
were superimposed by the CIA in 1978.

desperate attempt to stop the carnage by urging American military authorities to bomb the railroad center at Kaschau, which led from Hungary to Auschwitz, and to destroy the killing facilities themselves. Requests by Henry Morgenthau, Jr., secretary of the treasury, and John Pehle to the War Department were denied, allegedly due to limited resources and a lower priority. There can be little doubt, however, that the Allies possessed the capabilities to bomb Auschwitz, as evidenced by the aerial bombardment of the I. G. Farben plants at the Auschwitz-Monowitz complex as well as reconnaissance flights over the area.

The Hebrew Committee of National Liberation entreated the Joint Chiefs of Staff to threaten the Germans with the use of poison gas as long as they persisted in using poison gas to exterminate Jews. The request was denied by the Joint Chiefs of Staff, who contended that the Germans would know that the threat was an empty one, and if it were carried out, it would perhaps lead to an even greater loss of life.

The documents printed in this volume come from the Central Decimal File of the Department of State; the records of the War Refugee Board in the Franklin D. Roosevelt Library in Hyde Park, New York; the records of the Office of Strategic Services and the Headquarters of the Mediterranean Air Force as well as from those of the assistant secretary of war and the United States Joint Chiefs of Staff. One document was taken from the prosecution files of the Nuernberg Trials records. These documents include an exchange of telegrams between the American legation in Switzerland and the secretary of state concerning the rescue of Jews from Rumania. Some deal with the activities of the War Refugee Board, including minutes of meetings of the board with other agencies in Istanbul in the summer of 1944 and an index to rescue and relief licenses granted by the Department of the Treasury. Others record the futile attempts to persuade the War Department to bomb Auschwitz or the railway at Kaschau or to use poison gas against the exterminators. There is some documentation on the escape of the Weiss-Chorin families in exchange for most of their holdings. Transcripts of the interrogation of SS *Standartenfuehrer* Kurt Becher reveal strategies for the release or protection of Jews through negotiations with the SS itself.

Relief of the suffering of the Jews by the Allies and neutral nations commenced on an appreciable scale far too late, when most of the killings had already taken place. Nonetheless, the actions taken by the War Refugee Board, various Jewish agencies, and courageous individuals did save the lives of thousands of Jews.

John Mendelsohn

# SOURCE ABBREVIATIONS
## AND DESCRIPTIONS

**Nuernberg Document**

Records from five of the twenty-five Nuemberg Trials prosecution document series: the NG (Nuemberg Government) series, the NI (Nuemberg Industrialist) series, the NO (Nuemberg Organizations) series, the NOKW (Nuemberg Armed Forces High Command) series, and the PS (Paris-Storey) series. Also included are such Nuemberg Trials prosecution records as interviews, interrogations, and affidavits, excerpts from the transcripts of the proceedings, briefs, judgments, and sentences. These records were used by the prosecution staff of the International Military Tribunal at Nuemberg or the twelve United States military tribunals there, and they are part of National Archives Record Group 238, National Archives Collection of World War II War Crimes Records.

**OSS**

Reports by the Office of Strategic Services in National Archives Record Group 226.

**SEA**

Staff Evidence Analysis: a description of documents used by the Nuemberg prosecution staff. Although the SEA's tended to describe only the evidentiary parts of the documents in the summaries, they describe the document title, date, and sources quite accurately.

**State CDF**

Central Decimal File: records of the Department of State in National Archives Record Group 59, General Records of the Department of State.

**T 120**

Microfilm Publication T 120: records of the German foreign office received from the Department of State in Record Group 242, National Archives Collection of Foreign Records Seized, 1941– . The following citation system is used for National Archives

Microfilm Publications: The Microfilm Publication number followed by a slash, the roll number followed by a slash, and the frame number(s). For example, Document 1 in Volume I: T 120/4638/K325518— K325538.

## T 175

Microfilm Publication T 175: records of the Reich leader of the SS and of the chief of the German police in Record Group 242.

## U.S. Army and U.S. Air Force

Records relating to the attempts to cause the U.S. Army Air Force to bomb the extermination facilities at Auschwitz and the railroad center at Kaschau leading to Auschwitz, which are part of a variety of records groups and collections in the National Archives. Included are records of the United States Strategic Bombing Survey (Record Group 243), records of the War Refugee Board (Record Group 220), records of the Joint Chiefs of Staff, and other Army record collections.

## War Refugee Board

Records of the War Refugee Board, located at the Franklin D. Roosevelt Library in Hyde Park, New York. They are part of National Archives Record Group 220, Records of Temporary Committees, Commissions and Boards. Included in this category are the papers of Myron C. Taylor and Ira Hirschmann.

# CONTENTS

# Notes

1. *Document 2.* Gerhart Riegner was the secretary of the World Jewish Congress in Geneva. His report to the secretary of state pertaining to the Nazi extermination of Jews had considerable impact on the formation of the War Refugee Board.

2. *Document 3.* During the meetings of representatives of relief organizations at the office of the War Refugee Board in Istanbul during the three-month period from July 10 through October 9, 1944, the following organizations and individuals connected with them were frequently represented at the meetings:

*War Refugee Board*
Ira A. Hirschmann, chairman
Herbert Katzki, acting chairman
Irving H. Sherman

*Jewish Agency*
Mnachim Bader
Chaim Barlas
Dr. Eliash
J. Goldin
Eleazar Kaplan
Saul Meyerhoff
Venja Pomeraniec
Zeev Schind
Ehud Ueberall
David Zygmund

*American Jewish Joint Distribution Committee*
Mordecai Kessler
Charles Passman
Reuben Resnick
Joseph Schwartz

*Agudath Israel and Vaad Hahatzalah*
Jacob Griffel
Ludwig Kastner
Joseph Klarman

*HIAS-ICA Emigration Association (HICEM)*
David Schweitzer

*International Rescue and Relief Committee*
Leon Denenberg

*Emergency Committee for the Rescue of Jewish People in Europe*
Eri Jabotinsky

(COPY)

DEPARTMENT OF STATE
————————

Division of European Affairs

MEMORANDUM

May 17, 1943.

A-L - Mr. Long:

I have initialed this telegram since it proposes
to seek information from the American Legation at Bern
and does not envisage immediate action. I have certain
definite doubts about the subject matter referred to in
the telegram. In the first place questions of this sort
will properly fall within the competency of the Intergovernmental Committee. However, there are more serious
objections. There is no known present plan for the evacuation of children from Rumania to Palestine. The only plan
under active consideration is for the evacuation of 4,000
children from Bulgaria to Palestine and this, as you know,
will necessitate the use of the two Rumanian ships mentioned in Mr. Meltzer's memorandum of conversation. It
is still doubtful whether these ships will be obtained.
In addition the matter is vaguely phrased and it is believed that the sum desired by the American Jewish Congress may be for the purpose of a paying ransom. If so,
this is a question which would require special consideration.

The portion of this telegram which refers to France
is equally vague. It is not clear whether the children
mentioned are in France or outside. If they are in France
there is no indication as to the manner in which they are
to be rescued.

Eu:RBReams:BJS

PREPARING OFFICE
* WILL INDICATE WHETHER

Collect
Charge Department:
Full rate        {Full rate
Charge to        {Day letter
$                {Night letter

Full rate
Day letter
Night letter

Enciphered by ——————————— M., ——————— 19———

Sent by operator ——————————— M., ——————— 19———

U. S. GOVERNMENT PRINTING OFFICE   16—27293-1

TELEGRAM SENT

Department of State

Washington,

May 16, 1943.

TO BE TRANSMITTED
X   SECRET
    CONFIDENTIAL
    RESTRICTED
    CLEAR
PARAFOR
SECRET CODE

AMERICAN LEGATION,

BERN.

Your telegram 2461, April 20, 1943.

The telegram under reference has been discussed with Dr. Mahun Goldman of the American Jewish Congress. There are still certain financial questions which require clarification.

This telegram will present our interpretation of the proposed financial arrangements and will submit several related questions. Please report on the matter and discuss it with Dr. Reigner, the Geneva representative of the American Jewish Congress. Discussions with Reigner may be facilitated if you state that Dr. Goldman suggested that Reigner be consulted.

(1) With respect to Rumania it is assumed that necessary lei will be secured in the following manner: Remittances will be made by private groups in the United States to a Swiss bank. The remittances could be in favor of an agent

3

of the American Jewish Congress acceptable to this Government or in favor of a cooperative person in occupied territory. If the latter procedure were adopted, at the time the remittance was made it would be stipulated that no payment against the resulting accounts would be made by the Swiss bank, until after the war and until after an agent designated by the American Jewish Congress had approved such payment. The purpose of requiring this approval is to insure that any funds or services promised by the person in occupied territory had actually been furnished. It could also be stipulated that the accounts opened for the benefit of enemy nationals would not be assignable for the duration of the war. Where the remittance was made in favor of the agent of the American Jewish Congress he would establish accounts in Switzerland blocked for the duration of the war for the benefit of persons in occupied territory. If deemed desirable by you and the Department, the operations of this agent could be subjected to the advance approval of the Legation. These accounts would be established as compensation for services in occupied territory or for local currency

TO BE TRANSMITTED

SECRET
CONFIDENTIAL
RESTRICTED
CLEAR
PARTASE

PREPARING OFFICE
WILL INDICATE WHETHER

**TELEGRAM SENT**

# Department of State

*Washington,*

Collect { Full rate
{ Day letter
{ Night letter

Charge Department:
Full rate
Day letter
Night letter

Charge to
$

-3-

furnished there. Similar financial mechanics would be used for France.

(2) Is it contemplated that the official permission of the Rumanian Government for the departure of the refugees will be sought?

(3) Where is the camp in which the French children are lodged? We are not familiar with Camp Suez.

(4) Will the contemplated financial arrangements avoid benefit to the enemy for the duration of the war?

(4) In connection with the foregoing, there is no known plan for the evacuation of children from Rumania to Palestine. For your own information the only plan of this nature under active consideration envisages the transport of 4,500 children and adults from Bulgaria to Palestine. Although American interest in the evacuation of refugee children from France continues there are no definite plans at the present time for such action. Both this and the possibility of bringing children from Rumania are matters which will be considered in detail by the Intergovernmental Committee.

A prompt reply will be appreciated.

FF:BM:REH:SS

U. S. GOVERNMENT PRINTING OFFICE    10—25293-1

FW 862.4016/2269

PARAPHRASE OF TELEGRAM SENT

FROM: Secretary of State, Washington

TO: AMERICAN LEGATION, Bern

DATED: May 25, 1943, 10 a.m.

NUMBER: 1249

Reference your telegram of April 20, 1943, no. 2461. Discussions with reference to your telegram have been held with a representative of the American Jewish Congress, Dr. Mahun Goldman. Clarification of certain financial questions is still required.

Our interpretation of the proposed financial arrangements is presented in this telegram and several related questions are submitted. After discussion with Dr. Reigner, Geneva representative of the American Jewish Congress, kindly give consideration to and report on our interpretation and the relevant questions. It might facilitate discussion with Reigner if you mentioned that Dr. Goldman had proposed consultation with Reigner.

One. Regarding Rumania, it is presumed that the requisite lei will be acquired as follows: Private groups in the United States will make remittances to a bank in Switzerland. These remittances could be made out to a representative of the American Jewish Congress who is agreeable to this Government or to a resident of occupied territory who is willing to cooperate. In case the second method is employed, when the funds were remitted, stipulation would be made that the Swiss bank would effect no payment against the resultant accounts until approval of such payment had been given by an agent chosen by the American Jewish Congress and until after the war. The object in demanding this approval is to make certain that the person in occupied territory had actually furnished any funds or services promised. Stipulation could also be made that for the duration of the war the accounts opened in favor of enemy nationals could not be assigned.

If the funds were remitted to the agent of the American Jewish Congress, he would set up in Switzerland accounts in favor of individuals in occupied areas which accounts would be blocked for the duration of the war. If considered necessary by the Department and by you, the prior approval of the Legation could be required for the operation of these accounts. The establishment of these accounts would be in compensation of/currency provided in occupied areas or services rendered there. Financial method for France of a similar nature would be employed.

**local**

Two. Does the plan under consideration contemplate seeking the official consent of the Rumanian Government to the refugees' departure?

7

Three. What is the location of the French children's camp? Camp Suez is not familiar to us.

Four. With respect to the above, no plan is known for the removal from Rumania to Palestine of children. You are advised that the only plan of this kind being actively considered contemplates conveyance to Palestine from Bulgaria of 4,500 adults and children. No definitive plans for such action have been made at present, although American interest in the removal of refugee children from France continues. The Intergovernmental Committee will consider in detail both this matter and the possibility of bringing children from Rumania.

Please let us have a prompt reply.

HULL

FF:MW:EPF                                                                 5/28/43

**TELEGRAM RECEIVED**

BJR

This telegram must be
closely paraphrased be-
fore being communicated
to anyone. (C)

Secretary of State,

Washington.

3567, June 14, 1 p.m. (SECTION ONE)

Following based on statements made in interviews
with Doctor Riegner and memorandum submitted by him.

One. (a) reference numbered paragraph one of
Department's telegram. Riegner states that in contrast
to Poland food and clothing are relatively abundant
in Rumania but refugees lack funds and cannot purchase.
Riegner states that International Red Cross suggested
that instead of shipping food from limited Red Cross
supplies in Switzerland it would be simpler to purchase
food and clothing in Rumania for Jews concentrated in
trans-Nistria if funds could be made available there.
According to Riegner's plan Lei in Rumania would be
furnished to a relief agency by wealthy Rumanian
Jews from hidden resources. Counter value in dollars
or Swiss francs would be deposited in blocked account
either in Switzerland or in United States (Riegner pre-
fers Switzerland) which would be administered by agent
appointed by World Jewish Congress.

HARRISON

WWC

JUN 30 1943
MR. BRANDT

Dated June 14, 1943
Rec'd 5:03 p.m.

FROM

Department's telegram no. 1249, May 25.

# TELEGRAM RECEIVED

Bern

NMC

This telegram must be
closely paraphrased be**FROM** Dated June 14, 1945
fore being communicated
to anyone. (C)                    Rec'd 7:01 p.m.

Secretary of State,

Washington.

3567, June 14, 1 p.m., (SECTION TWO)

Swiss francs or dollars would not be deposited
in the name of beneficiaries (Russian Jews who
supplied lei) but agent would designate currently
or at the end of war persons to whom funds payable;
neither beneficiaries, assignees, heirs or others
having any claim on beneficiaries would be
permitted to draw on this account until after the
war. Exchange rates to be current black market rates
(Riegner states current rate 100 lei per 0.60 Swiss
francs).

(B)  Receipt of lei and disbursal for relief
purposes would be administered by Fildermann former
president of Jewish communities in Rumania. (Note--
According to recent German press report Fildermann
and wife sent to concentration camp Transnistria
under the direction of Fischer former representative
WJC in Rumania and Benvenisti former head Rumanian
Zionists

-2- #3567, June 14, 1 p.m., (SECTION TWO) from Berr

Zionists all Rumanians and if required under

supervision International Red Cross provided latter

agrees to plan.

NPL

HARRISON

# TELEGRAM RECEIVED

Bern

Dated June 14, 1943

Rec'd 7:12 p.m.

Secretary of State,

Washington,

3567, June 14, 1 p.m. (SECTION THREE)

(C) Riegner was asked whether payment of hidden funds to relief agency would not expose owners to confiscation and other penalties from the Rumanians. He replied that Rumania is "not like Switzerland" and that such matters can be "arranged".

Two. Reference numbered paragraphs two and four Department's telegram. Reigner stated approximately 30,000 Palestine entry permits available to Jews on the basis of British White Paper. WJC which hopes eventually to evacuate this number from Central Europe is currently working on project to evacuate 4000 children from Rumania and Bulgaria to Palestine by way of Turkey. Riegner states permission of Rumanian Government being sought by International Red Cross. According to Jewish Agency for Palestine Rumanian authorities have indicated that they are not opposed in principle to proposed emigration.

Major

-2- #3567, June 14, 1 p.m. from Bern

Major difficulties said to be securing Bulgarian transit permits and transportation through Turkey. With regard to latter Riegner believes negotiations under way in Turkey for chartering boat to transport refugees.

HARRISON

RR

# TELEGRAM RECEIVED

DLA

This telegram must be closely paraphrased before being communicated to anyone. (C)

FROM Bern

Dated June 14, 1943

Rec'd 7:25 p.m.

Secretary of State,

Washington.

3567, June 14, 1 p.m. (SECTION FOUR)

Number three. Reference numbered paragraph three. Riegner states camp (?)s (not Suez) located 40 kilometers west of Pauinbasses Pyrenees. It is for adults and not children.

Number four. Riegner states funds needed in France for favoring illegal departure of young Jews via Spain (cost per person for false papers and bribes estimated 15,000 and leaves 30,000 French francs) assisting Jewish political personalities who are hiding and for assistance to Jewish children being hidden by non-Jewish families. Riegner states that these activities up to present have been financed by relief funds transferred from United States prior to entry of war but resources of French Jewish underground organization now practically exhausted. He states Jarblum, President of Federation of French Jewish Societies, recently arrived in Switzerland

-2- #3567, June 14, 1 p.m. (SECTION FOUR) from Bern

Switzerland to endeavor arrange financing Jewish underground activities. Riegner proposes that persons in Switzerland (Jewish refugees or Swiss) who have funds in France release their French francs to the underground through intermediaries in return for payment in Swiss francs in Switzerland at black market rate.

HARRISON

WSB

# TELEGRAM RECEIVED

———————Bern

Ju
This telegram must be
closely paraphrased be-          Dated June 14, 1943
fore being communicated      **FROM**
to anyone.(C)                        Rec'd 7:08 p.m.

Secretary of State,

Washington.

3567, June 14, 1 p.m. (SECTION FIVE)

Riegner does not believe suppliers of

French francs would accept blocked dollars

or blocked Swiss francs in view of relatively

lively market for French francs. He states

no remittances of Swiss francs previously

granted dollars would be made to enemy

territory and that care would be taken that

dollar or Swiss franc recipients are not

working for or have any connection with Axis.

He states a monthly minimum budget of 15,000

to 20,000 Swiss francs necessary for these

purposes. Transactions would have to be

discreetly executed by persons trusted W.

J C and detailed accounting of disbursement

of funds in France impossible.

(Number five. Riegner and international

Red Cross endeavoring to obtain assurances

from

-2- 3567, June 14, 1 p.m.(SECTION FIVE) from Bern

from Germans which would permit despatch of food

parcels to G and also to towns in Upper Silesia

and Poland. Although outlook is not bright

Riegner proposes $10,000 be transmitted to him

by W J C, New York to be used immediately for

relief should Germans unexpectedly grant necessary

assurances.

HARRISON

# TELEGRAM RECEIVED

FROM:

WHC
This telegram must be
closely paraphrased be-
fore being communicated
to anyone. (C)

Dated June 14, 1943

Rec'd 7:14 p.m.

Secretary of State,

Washington.

3567, June 14, 1 p.m., (SECTION SIX)

7, Six. Riegner states he has been designated
as representative of World Jewish Congress
only but that connection between it and American
Jewish Congress is so close that he considers
himself as acting for both organizations. He
states he is under instructions from WJC New York
to obtain all possible information concerning
condition of Jews in Europe and that he accordingly
communicate with enemy territory through trusted
intermediaries for this purpose. (Legation would
appreciate being informed whether such communication
by WJC or AJC with persons in enemy territory
might require license under general ruling number
eleven).

Seven. The Legation has been informed by
the British Legation of the plan now under discussion
between London and Washington to effect relief
measures in

-2- #3567, June 14, 1 p.m., (SECTION SIX) from Bern

measures in occupied countries of the United
Nations by the disbursement of funds through the
United Nations missions in Switzerland, to the
International Red Cross for the purchase and
delivery of restricted food supplies to their
respective countries, distribution to be effected
by and through control of Red Cross. In view
of the rigorous control at present provided in the
proposed plan for relief in occupied Allied countries
the Legation presumes that Riegner plan for relief
and other activities in Rumania, France, Poland
and Upper Silesia will be considered as similar
to proposed plan for relief in occupied Allied
countries and in this connection will be discussed
with the British.

HARRISON

RR

18

# TELEGRAM RECEIVED

MIC

This telegram must be
closely paraphrased be- FROM Dated June 14, 1943
fore being communicated
to anyone. (C)          Rec'd 7:14 p.m.

--- --- Bern

Secretary of State,

Washington.

3567, June 14, 1 p.m. Section...

The method of utilizing funds and the extent of
relief or other activities are of course distinctly
different in the two plans. Also it will be
noted that independent agencies other than Red Cross
would in the Riegner plan play a major role in
Rumania and be employed exclusively in France. The
employment in Rumania of a separate agency for the
collection of funds, purchase and distribution of
supplies would appear to make close supervision of
these activities by the Red Cross extremely difficult
if not impossible and in the case of France as Riegner
states detailed control of the utilization of funds
disbursed would be impossible.

Eight. Reference one C above. It would appear
that the person in Rumania who would make lei
remittances plan to purchase their security through
payments to Rumania (and possibly German) officials.
If this assumption is correct funds so employed

might be

-2-    #3567, June 14, 1 p.m., from Bern

might be lei but it is more likely that officials
involved would demand share in dollar or Swiss
franc deposits. Even were the deposits theoretically
not assignable the possibility cannot be excluded that
such officials would be promised a share or that
they might even be designated as suppliers of
lei.

HARRISON

WSB

# TELEGRAM RECEIVED

FSH
This telegram must be
closely paraphrased be- FROM     Bern
fore being communicated          Dated  June 14, 1943
to anyone.  (C)                  Rec'd  7:17 p.m.

Secretary of State,

Washington,

3567, June 14, 1 p.m.  (SECTION EIGHT)

thus considered the Riegner plan offers many chances

of abuse through facilitation of flight of private

capital which might also include concealed enemy

funds.

Nine.  In view of the possibilities described in

eight above the inability of Legation to control

collection of funds in Rumania, the possible assignment

in Rumania of deposits in the United States, or

Switzerland, the lack of control over the disbursal

of Bolivars in France and in Rumania, supervision

of operation of accounts by the Legation, appears

to be impractical.

Ten.  Report on relation of International

Red Cross with foregoing will follow shortly.

(END OF MESSAGE)

HARRISON

RR

Min )s of an Informal Meeting )
held on Tuesday, July 1₂, 1944
at the Office of the O.W.I., Istanbul

of Representatives of Relief Organizations in Istanbul

Those present: I. A. Hirschmann, Herbert Katzki, Chaim Barlas, Joseph Klarman, Reuben Resnick, Ludwig Kastner, Eliezer Kaplan, Harry Viteles, Eri Jabotinsky, Izok Mitrani, Judah Magnes, Zeev Schind, David Schweitzer, J. Golden, Jacob Griffel, Joseph Schwartz, Leon Denenberg, Leder, Mnachim Bader, Moshe Averbuch, Akiba Levinsky.

The meeting was called to order at 4:45 p.m. by Mr. I. A. Hirschmann, as representative of the War Refugee Board.

At the outset, Mr. Hirschmann explained that the entire meeting was informal and off the record, and requested that no reports be made by the representatives of the respective organizations to their head offices until such time as definite accomplishments could be reported.

Mr. Hirschmann explained that he had called the meeting pursuant to suggestions made by Ambassador Steinhardt at an informal luncheon conference, which he arranged in Ankara on July 2, 1944. A number of people now present had likewise been present at Ambassador Steinhardt's luncheon.

For the benefit of those who were not there on July 2, Mr. Hirschmann recapitulated briefly some of the things concerning which the Ambassador had spoken to the organization representatives. The Ambassador urged that the relief organizations coordinate their efforts for the rescuing of persecuted peoples. Independent action, such as competitive bidding for ships, independent demarches with various authorities without regard to what others might have done before, conflicting reports and projects, all made very difficult the work of the Embassy in its relationships with the individual organizations, with Washington and with officials in Turkey. All this had an effect disadvantageous to those whom the several agencies tried to serve. The Ambassador had, therefore, suggested that the work of the organizations, all of which was directed to the same end, be coordinated, perhaps through the establishment of a committee upon which would be represented all the agencies in Turkey engaged in refugee relief work. However, recognizing that such a committee might be too large and unwieldy, the Ambassador had suggested, further, that a smaller operating committee be created which would be responsible for the execution of the day-to-day work involved in the rescue and relief programs. The Ambassador also proposed that both committees operate under the leadership of the War Refugee Board and its special representative, Mr. Hirschmann.

In accordance with the Ambassador's suggestion, Mr. Hirschmann had called today's meeting together. Furthermore, he wished to take advantage of the presence in Istanbul of Dr. Magnes, Dr. Schwartz and Mr. Kaplan, all of whom had had wide experience, and whose judgment and advice would be most helpful.

Mr. Hirschmann went on to explain the great and sympathetic interest of the United States Government in refugee rescue activities, which had been exemplified in part through the creation of the War Refugee Board. Mr. Hirschmann had been sent to Turkey by the Board both to initiate rescue projects and to assist the agencies already in the field in those programs upon which they were working. He referred to the many ways in which the Board can be helpful to the private agencies, and called upon them to make use of him to the fullest extent where his aid and that of the Board might be of assistance. He briefly outlined the problems in Istanbul and Bucharest, the point of origin of many of the refugees now passing through Turkey, and then asked for suggestions from the floor as to the manner in which the work in both centers might be coordinated in order to achieve maximum results.

Dr. Magnes stated that he had studied the situation in Turkey at first hand for a number of days, and had spoken with a great many people. He felt that, although there may be room for improvement in the work up to this point, it was wise for

-3-

all to withhold judgment at the present time. It is his own feeling, however, that accomplishments have been very great, and the work of the organizations very much better than he had been led to expect. Dr. Wagnes then outlined briefly what he had learned during his various conversations concerning the position of Jewish people in the Balkan countries, and emphasized the scope of the problem which, in his opinion, made all the more necessary concerted action on the part of the relief organizations. He recommended, therefore, that the representatives of the various organizations form themselves into an advisory committee which would meet from time to time to report, advise and suggest programs and plans of action to a smaller actions committee, to be created, which would conduct the day-to-day work. This smaller committee, however, neednot take instructions from the larger advisory committee, although being guided by it. He asked for coordination and cooperation behind the War Refugee Board and Mr. Hirschmann. Concerning the distribution of places on the boats coming from Rumania, he suggested as a solution to the problems in Bucharest that the passengers be designated, one-half by the Zionist representative, and one-half by an apolitical person.

Dr. Schwartz stated that thought should be given at this meeting to the mechanics to be set up, and not to the designation of responsibilities. He agreed with what Dr. Magnes had said, but did not like the concept of an advisory committee. In his opinion, there should be general discussions and interchange of information and views among the agency representatives, but the representatives should not be crystallized into a formal advisory group. He preferred that everything be done on an informal basis. Dr. Schwartz then made the following suggestions:

1) The representative of the War Refugee Board should call the people together whenever he thinks they should meet, or when their advice is necessary. He pointed out that more formal organization might result in complications arising out of the

-4-

fact that number of the representatives, being Palestinian, were British subjects, and consequently it might be embarrassing for them if they were tied up too closely with an American organization, the War Refugee Board. Their actions might be construed as being subject to American control.

2) The Joint Distribution Committee could not formally tie itself up with a mixed group, which included agencies interested not only in relief, but also in political work. The JDC is non-political in character, and is interested solely in humanitarian work. Therefore, it does not want to, nor can it, become involved in political matters. However, the JDC would be very happy to meet with representatives of any organization either at the call of Mr. Hirschmann or at that of the other organizations if they think it desirable.

He recommended, therefore, that the small working committee be made up of the representatives of agencies effectively working in the field of rescuing people or the relief of people in occupied countries. The JDC would be very glad to participate in such a committee, provided its make-up were satisfactory to it.

As Dr. Schwartz saw it, the work in Istanbul divided itself into three sections:

a) The rescue of people by providing transportation.

b) The relief of people in occupied areas.

c) Providing for rescued people while in transit through Turkey.

He suggested that the smaller committee be made up of representatives of the Jewish Agency, the JDC, and "minority" groups, even though their participation in the work is small because they are nevertheless interested. He suggested a working committee of a maximum of five people, keeping the number small for the sake of getting things done.

Mr. Kaplan opposed the conception of an advisory committee, and thought that such meetings should be in the form of conferences, as more closely characterizing their work. Of

course, the principle of all the organizations is to save as
many people as possible, and the function of the conference
would be to put workable ideas before the group. He touched
briefly on the matter of the selection of emigrants, and
pointed out that some of the organizations, such as the Jewish
Agency, have responsibilities toward Palestine which must guide
them in making selections. Therefore, this question cannot
be regarded as a simple one. He recommended that discussions
for the improvement and expansion of the work be taken up
immediately after today's meeting and that the organizations
intensify their efforts.

Mr. Barlas suggested omitting all discussions having to do
with the refugee position in Bucharest, and that this meeting
should confine itself to the question of organization. He
thought that the War Refugee Board should call meetings of
representatives whenever three organizations requested them.

Mr. Jabotinsky stated that he had been studying the situation for upwards of two months and that during this period he
had undertaken no projects at all. In his opinion the cooperation offered by the American Embassy has been good, and he
expressed his expectation that, with the presence of Mr. Hirschmann, the cooperation extended through the Embassy and other
channels will be even better. He also thought that the rescue
work done by Messrs. Schind, Averbuch, and others whom he
mentioned by name, had been excellent. He thought, however,
that the question of the distribution of places on boats cannot
be the subject of discussion, as this is related to that of
responsibility for determining who is or who is not suitable
material for Palestine. He thought it important that, in setting
up the smaller committee, due regard should be had for assisting
non-Jewish refugees. He was glad the group had met, since it
brought the relief and rescue work under United States Government auspices.

At this point, Mr. Hirschmann in response to a question

defined the purposes of two proposed committees as follows:
the large group would be informative, and the smaller group
would make operating decisions. Mr. Denenberg was of the
opinion that the time had arrived when all the organizations
should cooperate and work together, and that everyone should
participate in the work, avoiding "monopoly."

Mr. Kaplan suggested that Mr. Hirschmann assume the
responsibility for designating the smaller operating committee,
to consist of up to five persons, not counting Mr. Hirschmann,
who would serve as chairman. The meeting unanimously accepted
this proposal.

Mr. Hirschmann accepted this responsibility, saying that
he will designate a committee after full discussions with
those present.

The meeting was adjourned at 6:15.

# Minutes of an Informal Meeting

## of the Operating Group of Relief Organizations

### held at the American Consulate, Istanbul

#### July 17, 1944

Those present: I. A. Hirschmann, Herbert Katzki, for War Refugee Board; Joseph Schwartz and Reuben Resnick, American Joint Distribution Committee; Eleazar Kaplan, Chaim Barlas, and Zeev Schind, Jewish Agency; David Schweitzer, Hias-Ica Immigration Association.

The meeting was called to order by Mr. Hirschmann at 4:15 p.m. He welcomed the representatives present, and stated that he is not regarding those present as forming either a formal or informal committee, but his only desire was to get work done; and the characterization of the meetings, of which this was the first, can be developed later.

Rumania. Mr. Schind advised the group that there are still three Turkish boats at Constanza, and the Smirni, a Greek boat, waiting to carry refugees from Constanza to Istanbul. The last news he had was to the effect that the Smirni has permission to carry people from Constanza and is now awaiting the completion of some technical details before undertaking its voyage. The three Turkish boats are ready to leave at any time, but in addition there are three Bulgarian boats in Varna, the Milca, the Vita, and the Pirin, which likewise can be sent from Varna to Constanza to carry people to Istanbul. The Milca has definite permission to go to Constanza for this purpose. The question now arises as to whether or not any of the three boats should be sent to Constanza to be kept there in the event that emigration again becomes possible. In his opinion, the Milca should be sent to

Minutes          -2-          July 17, 1944

Constanza, leaving the other two boats at Varna to carry refugees from Bulgaria, should this become possible. It was his view that, because of the reported uncertain political situation in Rumania, it might be well to concentrate there the largest number of available boats, to move people as rapidly as opportunity afforded. In any event, even if emigration by sea from Bulgaria should become possible, it would take several weeks before arrangements could be made for filling two boats, so that the third, the Milca, could be spared. In addition, the shipping situation in Bulgaria is not as acute as it is in Rumania, since there is a number of small boats going to Varna each week from Istanbul, to carry merchandise to Bulgaria.

Mr. Kaplan stated that there was some difficulty with regard to the Smirni. Mr. Schind and his friends say that the departure of the boat is dependent only upon the preparation of passenger lists. According to Mr. Zissu, it is not possible for the Smirni to leave at all. Mr. Kaplan stated that two cables had been sent to Zissu, stating that the Smirni must sail, and indicating that perhaps it might be advisable to condition any discussions concerning the Rumanian boats upon the departure of the Smirni. He asked whether it would be possible, through fresh channels, to determine what is holding up the Smirni, either through Fildermann, or through channels available to Mr. Hirschmann. It should also be determined whether the discussion of Rumanian boats has any reality, or whether the entire discussion is without foundation.

In Mr. Schind's opinion, and according to information he has, it would take at least two months to put the Rumanian ships in physical condition to travel to Istanbul.

Mr. Resnick stated that it is possible to send additional Turkish boats directly from Istanbul to Rumania, and suggested that perhaps the Turkish minister, who had just returned to Rumania, might be helpful. He foresees no difficulties in obtaining the necessary Turkish permits for the boats to go directly to Constanza. Such boats could be made available through the same channels as are those now being used.

Discussion then ensued as to the person or agency responsible for the filling of the ships in Constanza. The discussion developed that it was entirely unclear as to whether this responsibility lay with Zissu, the Rumanian government, both together, or with the organization Orat, which has prepared the boats which thus far have come from Constanza.

Mr. Kaplan reported that Zissu stated explicitly and Fildermann in part that, as the three Turkish boats now in Constanza have left, only Rumanian ships can be used for carrying refugees.

Discussion was then had as to the advisability of sending additional Turkish boats to Constanza at the present time, despite Zissu's messages concerning Rumanian ships, on the grounds that the actual presence of additional boats might exert sufficient pressure to make them acceptable for use. No decision was taken as to this. The question then arose as

Minutes      -4-      May 17, 1944

to the manner in which pressure might be applied on Zissu to remove whatever obstacles he may be creating to the movement of the ships, if, indeed, he is creating any. Mr. Kaplan stated that he will write a strong letter to Mr. Zissu on the subject, of which a copy will be made available to Mr. Hirschmann. Mr. Hirschmann would consider whether or not, and by what means, he would attempt the same thing.

Mr. Hirschmann reported that he had written to Charge d'Affaires Kelley concerning the Turkish ship Anadolu, which could go to Constanza if Turkish permission were received. He had asked Mr. Kelley to follow this up with the Foreign Office. It was decided that Mr. Barlas and Mr. Resnick should make inquiry into the general question of sending further Turkish ships from Istanbul to Constanza with Turkish permission.

Bulgaria. Mr. Schind suggested that steps be taken to arrange for the release of people now in Bulgaria, of whom a large number are ready to depart for transport by sea to Istanbul, in the same manner as do those coming here from Rumania. Turkish boats are available for this purpose, since several go to Bulgaria each week with cargo.

Mr. Kaplan's information is that Bulgaria does not oppose the exit of Jewish people, but that it appears that the Turkish consul has been obstructing it. He suggested that Mr. Hirschmann have the Turkish Foreign Office inform the consulate in Bulgaria that the Turkish government is ready to close its eyes to the fact that people arrive by ship to Turkey en route to Palestine, without being in possession of Turkish transit visas. Apparently, the Turkish consul has informed the Bulgarian government that he opposes the departure of Jewish people to Istanbul under these circumstances. In addition, the Turkish Foreign Office should advise the Bulgarian government of its attitude concerning the arrival in Istanbul of people without Turkish transit visas.

Dr. ~~Schweitzer~~ Schwartz suggested pursuing the question of increasing land traffic from Bulgaria to Turkey by increasing from nine to twenty the number of transit visas authorized weekly for Sofia. An additional argument might be used on the grounds that no refugees are arriving from Hungary, for which nine visas weekly had likewise been authorized.

Mr. Hirschmann referred to the reluctance of the Bulgarian government to permit refugees to come to Istanbul on the grounds that they are subjected to too many G-2 investigations upon their arrival here. He thought it might be helpful if assurances could be given to the Bulgarian government that no such interviews would take place in Istanbul, so far as refugees were concerned.

Mr. Hirschmann stated that, in a memorandum which he had prepared for transmission to the Bulgarian government, he had suggested that priority be given to children and young people, if emigration from Bulgaria were permitted. He had done this in order to overcome Bulgarian objections to emigration on the grounds of G-2 interviews.

es     -6-     July 17,1944

Dr. Schwartz opposed emigration limited to specific categories, since more people than just children and youths want to leave Bulgaria, and their departure may not be opposed.

Hungary. Mr. Kaplan reported that further clandestine movement of refugees in Hungary to Rumania, according to information he had just received, depended upon finances. He, in behalf of the Jewish Agency, and Dr. Schwartz Schneider, are consulting together on this question. Dr. Schweitzer indicated that finances provided no problem at the moment.

Mr. Kaplan thought it important that movement from Hungary to Rumania be augmented, through strengthening of appropriate local organizations. Although Rumania officially has decreed a death sentence to anyone assisting such movement, in reality they apparently are willing to take no notice of it. Naturally, complications arise in Bucharest, where decision must be taken as to whether available places on boats should be given to people already in Rumania or those coming from Hungary, since all are anxious to leave. Mr. Schind reported that there are already fifteen hundred Hungarian refugees in Rumania who could be brought to Istanbul, were shipping facilities available.

Mr. Schind referred also to the group of six hundred Jugoslavian Jews in Hungary, who are in possession of Swiss Schützenpässe, and which might be regarded as a group for emigration. Apparently, a time-limit of July 1st for moving them out of Hungary has been extended to August 1st, and the matter should be followed up.

Mr. Kaplan referred to a scheme put forward by the Swedish

minister in Budapest, by which Swedish visas of a limited number and to certain categories of Jewish people might be issued, if a guarantee is provided the Swedish government ^that such people would be removed from Sweden within three years' time. This matter should also be looked into and followed up.

Mr. Kaplan referred to a letter he had just received from Budapest which indicated that tens of thousands of persons could be saved if the cost of their maintenance could be taken over. He is pursuing the matter, in order to secure more information.

Mr. Hirschmann referred to his conversation with Mr. Griffel, and advised the group that the War Refugee Board, as representing the United States Government, has adopted the principle that it cannot discourage the sending of ships by individual private agencies, if they have responsible projects in hand. He had tried to concentrate all ship questions into one channel, but apparently all necessary agreements could not be achieved.

Both Mr. Kaplan and Dr. Schwartz expressed their approval of the idea of periodic conferences similar to the present one, and felt that much good could come of them in terms of cooperation and coordination of the work. Each felt that better understand-ing and cooperation had been reached in behalf of their respective organizations as a result of their personal talks in Istanbul.

Mr. Hirschmann explained the presence of Mr. Schweitzer, saying that he had been invited in order to present the point

ates          -8-          July 17, 1944

of view of an outsider, that is, one who is neither Jewish Agency nor Joint Distribution Committee. He will be invited to subsequent meetings.

The meeting adjourned at 6:15 p.m.

M I N U T E S

of a Meeting of the Operating Committee

of Relief Organizations

July 24, 1944

---

Mr. Katzki opened the meeting by recapitulating briefly some of the problems which had arisen since the last meeting on July 17. He advised the group also that Mr. Hirschmann had left for Ankara this morning, to take up there some of the pressing problems which had arisen, and which could best be handled from the capital. Among these, briefly, were the increase in the number of authorized transit visas for Buda-pest, Bucharest and Sofia from 9 to 20 weekly; the permit for the SS <u>Anadolu</u>; the opening up of the Turkish border; the movement of boats from Bulgarian ports; the offer of the Swedish government with regard to the admission into Sweden of Jewish people from Hungary having Swedish contacts; and so forth. Mr. Katkzi stated that Mr. Hirschmann was expected back in Istanbul towards the end of the week.

Mr. Schweitzer raised the question as to whether or not the boats departing from Bulgaria might not go directly to Haifa, to avoid transportation complications through Istanbul. Mr. Schind pointed out that the boats in Buggas were of Bulgar-ian registry, and consequently could not sail into Palestinian waters.

Mr. Schind raised the question again of the opposition on the part of Bulgarian authorities to releasing people on the grounds that several governments had been questioning refugees for the purpose of obtaining military information. It was the

consensus of opinion that this problem would have to be met in a practical way, and that it was probably the Turkish authorities who were meant. As to this, there may be nothing one can do, especially since, even when the refugees are kept out in the harbor to avoid public contact, the Turkish police accompany the trains down to the Syrian border.

Mr. Schind mentioned that it would be desirable if the Turkish Foreign Office could advise the Bulgarian government concerning its attitude about admitting people into Turkey who were not in possession of Turkish transit visas, also the need for having the Foreign Office advise the Turkish consulate in Burgas of this attitude. Mr. Katzki advised the group that this was one of the problems which Mr. Hirschmann would take up in Ankara.

Mr. Schind advised the meeting that the individual letters addressed to Mr. Zissu by Mr. E. Kaplan and Mr. Hirschmann were sent away in due course. Telegraphic communications with Rumania remain poor, but within the past few days two or three cables were received in Istanbul by various agencies with representatives in Bucharest. There is no new information concerning the departure of the small Turkish boats, but according to Mr. Schind's information the passenger lists, for some unknown reason, had not yet been prepared, and submitted to the Bulgarian authorities, up to the end of last week. There is no explanation, therefore, and Mr. Schind has sent a strong message to Bucharest on the subject.

Mr. Resnick, on behalf of Mr. Schind and himself, reported that up to the present time no steps had been taken with regard to the obtention of additional Turkish boats in Istanbul, for which, according to Mr. Resnick, as stated at the last meeting, permits for the trip to Constanza were already available. Upon discussion it developed that permits for boats had not actually been issued. Instead, there exists merely an assurance given by the Ministry of Communications to Mr. Saracoglu, who heads up the steamship agency with which the Jewish Agency had been operating, to the effect that permits would be issued for small Turkish boats, if and when they are requested. It would be necessary, of course, to give the names of the boats in advance, and other details concerning the projected voyage. Under the circumstances, and since there are already Turkish boats in Constanza which are not moving, there would be no point in sending additional boats at this time. Mr. Schind stated, however, that, should large numbers of refugees become actual, Turkish boats having necessary permits could be in Constanza in a matter of days.

Mr. Schind reported that another Turkish boat, the Salah-Aladin, on its own initiative had sailed from Burgas to Constanza to pick up refugees, and that it at present is also available.

Mr. Barlas reported that a group of forty children, under the children's scheme, is expected to leave Sofia on July 29.

It appears that the technical difficulties involved in meeting the British requirement of Swiss Legation identifying endorsements on the passports of all children coming from Sofia have been met. Mr. Barlas has telegraphed to Sofia to make sure that the necessary instructions had been received by the Swiss Legation.

There is no doubt concerning the probability of the departure of this group. In addition, there are three more groups of 75 each, totaling 210 children and 15 escorts, which will be coming out from Sofia during August. In his opinion, there is no need for following up the matter at this time, as the technical questions have already been met.

Referring to the previous meeting, Mr. Resnick reported that Dr. Schwartz, while he was still in Istanbul, requested the JDC in New York to make a one-time grant of $500,000 to be transmitted to Mr. Saly Meyer in Switzerland, to be held at the disposition of the Budapest committee, consisting of Messrs. Freudiger, Blum, etc. These funds would be used for the maintenance of Jewish people in Hungary. In addition, a request was transmitted to New York for a budget of $360,000 per month for this purpose.

Mr. Berlas reported on his discussions with the Hungarian minister to Turkey concerning the emigration to Palestine of the holders of Palestine certificates, and other questions. The substance of his discussions is set forth in a note regarding the situation of the Jews in Hungary, which was circulated at the meeting, and to which reference is made.

In connection with the number of Palestine certificates available, Mr. Berlas stated that certified lists, containing 8200 cases, have already been sent to the Swiss Ministry in Budapest. In addition, there are available lists bearing 3000 names, which are in process of certification and transmission. Additional names are being received every day from a number of sources. These lists cover between twenty and twenty-five thousand people, as a certificate is good for an entire family. Mr. Barlas stated that the question has not arisen concerning the number of certificates which might be made available for Budapest. The British have certified all lists submitted by the Jewish Agency, and the Agency will continue submitting lists as long as it can.

During the discussions regarding the delivery of individual confirmations to the people in Hungary, for whom Palestine visas had been authorized, the following emerged:

(1) The Jewish Agency has used three separate means to place individual confirmations into the hands of the benefic- iaries: a) directly to the individuals, through certain facili- ties; b) through the Swiss Legation in Budapest, and c) through the Papal Nuncio in Budapest. The chief difficulty in accom- plishing this has been the lack of the present address of the individuals concerned. Efforts are being made to correct address lists to the fullest extent possible.

(2) It has been rumored that confirmations of Palestine certificates have been issued locally in Hungary by unauthorized persons. Mr. Barlas had heard about these rumors, and steps are being taken to control this situation.

(3) As many people to whom Palestine certificates have been authorized have already been deported, the question arose as to the manner in which these people might be located and brought back to Budapest for purposes of emigration. It was agreed that the International Red Cross was probably the best agency for dealing with this matter. At the present time, according to Mr.

*40*

Schweitzer (sic) me
that [illegible] who had
raised the question about
new emigration
I came him the
British transportation
his request

Barlas, the International Red Cross, however, has no jurisdiction in Poland. Mr. Barlas stated further that he would make inquiry [See writing?] to see in what way the Swedish authorities can be helpful in this connection. Mr. Katzki stated that the WRB would concern itself with this question.

(4) There was a difference of opinion as to whether or not certificates issued to residents of Slovakia were covered by the statement given Mr. Barlas concerning the emigration of Palestine certificate holders from Hungary, and as to whether or not separate Slovakian exit visas would have to be secured. In Jewish Agency procedure, Slovakia is considered the same as Hungary, and according to Mr. Barlas Slovakian exit permits are not necessary. Other opinions expressed were that Slovakia, technically, is independent, under which circumstance separate steps might perhaps have to be taken for Slovakian visa holders. Mr. Barlas will make inquiry into this situation, as will Mr. Schweitzer, who originally brought the matter up.

Referring to the implementation of the Hungarian policy, it was the opinion of Mr. Schind that the same channels through which pressure was brought to bear upon Hungary to permit the departure of Jewish people, should be used to cause the Hungarian government to grant transit facilities. In his view, efforts made only in Turkey would be insufficient, and the present political situation must be exploited to the utmost. In addition, since the announcement of Hungarian policy, according to Istanbul newspapers, was made through the International Red Cross, this organization evidently had interested itself in the matter.

Consequently, the International Red Cross should be approached to concern itself with questions of transportation, documentation, transit visas, etc. It is most important at this stage, with mass emigration becoming more and more of a possibility, that sure and rapid communication with Budapest and Bucharest and Sofie be available. Mr. Schind suggested that the WRB discuss with the International Red Cross, the Swedish Legation, or the Swiss Legation, the possibility of making use of their facilities for courier service. Facilities now available are not certain enough to handle the many day-to-day questions which arise.

Mr. Katzki introduced the question of transporting refugees down the Danube from Budapest. Mr. Schind reported that six months ago the British Naval Attache authorized the Turks to send a barge up the Danube. There was no way to do this, however, because of the Germans, and because the Danube is a military line and because of the mines in the river. At that time, when the Jewish Agency groups had considered this possibility, it was unfeasible. While Mr. Schind does not think that this situation has changed substantially, he nevertheless will get in touch with his representatives in Hungary, Rumania, and Bulgaria to re-examine this possibility. Although there may be empty boats now coming down the Danube from Budapest, the fact that the river is a military zone precludes any transport of passengers on such boats.

Mr. Katzki raised the question of the organization of the reception, care while in Istanbul, and onward transportation of refugees who may be coming by railroad or sea from the Balkans. He suggested that perhaps steps could be

42

taken more efficiently to handle the refugees while in transit in Istanbul. There was general discussion on this subject, and it was agreed that the group present today would meet again on Friday, July 28, at 3 o'clock, to consider this one problem alone. There being no further business, the meeting was adjourned at 6 p.m.

The meeting took place in the office of Mr. Herbert Katzki in the Perapalas Hotel, Istanbul. Those present were: Herbert Katzki, Zeev Schind, Chaim Barlas, Reuben Resnick, and David Schweitzer.

43

M I N U T E S

of a Meeting of the Operating Committee

of Relief Organizations

July 31, 1944

The meeting took place in the office of Mr. I. A. Hirschmann at the American Consulate General, Istanbul. Those present were: I. A. Hirschmann, Herbert Katzki, Zeev Schind, Chaim Barlas, David Schweitzer, and Reuben Resnick.

I. Mr. Schind reported that, according to a telegram dated July 27 received in Istanbul from Mr. Pandelis in Bucharest, the Turkish consul in Bucharest was creating difficulties in clearing the three Turkish boats in Constanza, because of the absence of Turkish transit visas. Schind judged that apparently everything was in order for the departure of the ships, excepting for Turkish consulate consent. He thought it important that the Turkish Foreign Office send fresh instructions to the Turkish consulate in Bucharest of a positive nature, to the effect that the boats could be cleared even though the passengers were not in possession of transit visas.

Mr. Hirschmann explained that, at his request, Mr. Simond of the International Red Cross had sent a strong telegram to Mr. Kolb, Intercross representative in Bucharest, advising him about the order for the return of Turkish boats to Turkish waters, and impressing upon him that these boats are not to return to Istanbul without passengers. Mr. Simond also tried to reach Bucharest by telephone, but was unable to do so. The approval of the Foreign Office of the arrival of the Turkish boats carrying passengers without transit visas has been made clear. Ambassador Steinhardt had this clarified with Mr. Saracoglu of the Foreign Office, and Mr. Kelley interceded on three separate occasions on the matter. Mr. Saracoglu assured the Embassy that the necessary steps had been taken vis-a-vis the Turkish consulate. Nevertheless, Mr. Hirschmann has brought to Mr. Kelley's attention the information contained in Pandelis' telegram.

To make a fresh effort to determine the situation, it was agreed that Mr. Hirschmann would ask Mr. Simond to have Mr. Kolb find out whether there has been any mix-up in connection with the instructions in Bucharest.

II. There was a brief discussion of the possible effect upon rescue work if a break between Germany and Turkey, about which so many rumors are now current in Istanbul, should take place. It was the consensus of opinion that should this occur, boat movement to Istanbul would be cut off. In this connection Mr. Resnick reported that after Wednesday, August 2, it will no longer be possible to use German freight cars to move freight into occupied territories from Istanbul.

III. Mr. Hirschmann outlined briefly and in confidence the gist of his discussions with Mr. Balabanoff. He mentioned the letter addressed by Mr. Balabanoff addressed to Mr. Simond, in which four points were made: (1) that the abuses directed against the Jewish people in Bulgaria will cease; (2) the government will assist in the emigration of Jewish people; (3) a committee of Jewish people had been called in in Sofia to help in the foregoing; and (4) the present government is in disagreement with the policies of the previous government concerning Jewish people. At the present time it is not possible to revoke the two basic anti-Jewish laws, but ways and means for doing so in due course will be considered.

Mr. Hirschmann explained that Mr. Kelley had a conference with Mr. Saracoglu, who said that he would like to see a continuous movement of ships between Bulgaria and Istanbul, and spoke in terms of a "bridge of ships". Mr. Saracoglu does not like the sporadic ship movements, and would prefer to have them arrive according to some schedule, so that the necessary technical arrangements for onward railroad transportation from Istanbul can be made.

In the discussion which followed concerning Bulgarian emigration, Mr. Hirschmann pressed for all possible steps to augment the movement, as in his opinion Bulgaria today is one country from which substantial numbers of people can be evacuated and for which the groundwork has been adequately laid in Istanbul, and can be controlled from there. Mr. Barlas indicated that he had learned, very indirectly, that the Turkish government is considering the publication of an unofficial communique on the subject of Turkish transit facilities; however, he had no further information or details on the subject. Mr. Schind received a message today that a man who was sent to Bulgaria two months ago in connection with the organization of transportation, will be back in Istanbul tomorrow. He is well-informed as to the boat situation in Varna, and it should be possible to obtain accurate and full information from him.

This man has been in touch with Joseph Levy of the Jewish community of Rousse, which has been charged with responsibility for emigration work with Jewish people from Bulgaria. In his opinion, the Bulgarian boats now in Varna will be able to come through.

Mr. Barlas reported that the next group of 75 children from Bulgaria is expected in Istanbul on August 10.

IV. Mr. Schind raised the question of the chartering of Turkish boats by Mr. Griffel for the evacuation of refugees in whom the organizations which he represents are interested. In his opinion, the War Refugee Board had no right to authorize Mr. Griffel to send a telegram to Bucharest in the name of Mr. Hirschmann to the effect that all Jewish refugees arriving in Istanbul would be able to secure Palestine visas. In the first place, it is only the Jewish Agency which has the right to determine who shall and who shall not receive such certificates. In the second place, Mr. Griffel's entrance into the field of shipping complicates the market in Istanbul, and confuses issues in Bucharest, should more than one agency be involved in the embarkation of refugees from that point. It is possible to secure all boats which might be needed. Essentially, Mr. Griffel wants to secure a larger percentage for Agudath Israel people in the allotment of places on those boats which sail from Constanza, and in fact had proposed to Mr. Schind that he would want "half a ship" for his protegees.

In response, Mr. Hirschmann explained the War Refugee Board policy at the time it encouraged Mr. Griffel to undertake steps for separate ships. Mr. Griffel was informed that the Board had no objection if he was able to secure boats in an orderly way, and that the Board, not being interested in the age, politics, or anything else of people to be rescued, would encourage any organization which put forward a reasonable scheme. Before Mr. Griffel was thus advised, Mr. Hirschmann had discussed the matter with Dr. Joseph Schwartz and Mr. Eliezer Kaplan in Istanbul. Furthermore, this statement of policy had been reported to Washington, which had approved thereof. Consequently, there can be no question of withdrawing this statement of policy.

Mr. Resnick agreed with Mr. Hirschmann's viewpoint, and mentioned that Mr. Griffel had approached him today, advising him that negotiations for a vessel have been undertaken and requesting a cash advance in this connection. Mr. Resnick desired an opinion as to whether Griffel's action would impede the program in Constanza.

Mr. Schind stated that, if it is Mr. Griffel's intention to send ships to Constanza, he would immediately telegraph to Bucharest to the effect that no Agudath Israel people were to be embarked on vessels sponsored by the Jewish Agency. When Dr. Wagnes and Dr. Schwartz were in Istanbul, it was decided that the Jewish Agency could not give the necessary confirmations to Bucharest which Mr. Griffel requested, and which had been given indirectly by Mr. Hirschmann. It was agreed at that time that there must not be more than one organization in Rumania dealing with questions of shipping.

Mr. Hirschmann reaffirmed the Board policy as he had stated it and advised Schind not to send the telegram he proposed.

Should he do so, Mr. Hirschmann would want to know about it so that he in turn can advise Washington. In the meanwhile, he thought it more important to move the four ships now in Constanza, which apparently are blocked there, rather than to worry about the effect of sending other ships there at some future time.

**V.** Discussion was had concerning the proposed project of Mr. Jabotinsky to send a wooden boat from Istanbul up the Danube to Budapest. Mr. Hirschmann outlined in some detail the project as it was presented, and advised the group that he had informed Mr. Jabotinsky that he could not support the scheme, as it seems today to be unfeasible, and required more information. However, he did not shut the door on the matter. The Jabotinsky project differed from Griffel's project in that the latter seemed feasible and worthy of encouragement, whereas the former at the moment did not seem feasible. Mr. Schind and Mr. Barlas jointly explained their contacts with Mr. Kazim and the circumstances under which they were placed in contact with him. They stated that their relationships with Kazim on a Danubian project antedated Jabotinsky's, and that two possibilities were being considered: (a) the despatch of a Turkish boat from Istanbul (for which Mr. Kazim thinks permission could not be secured under present circumstances), and (b) the use of Danubian barges to be secured in Rumania or in Budapest. Mr Schind explained to Mr. Kazim that he will have to make up his mind as to whom he wants to work for, Jabotinsky or the Jewish Agency. If the latter, this must be exclusive. Negotiations with Kazim have reached an advanced stage, but he has not yet advised the Jewish Agency explicitly that he will confine himself to their service. Mr. Kazim is

50

expected to leave Istanbul either the end of this week or the beginning of next week.

Mr. Resnick reported that the Antalya Agency is investigating the position in Budapest in behalf of Triton Vapeur. He raised the question as to whether it might not be sound for the Jewish Agency to send additional ships to Constanza, if it seems expedient for.Mr. Griffel to do so. The JDC had been in a position to despatch boats with necessary permission, but had refrained from doing so in order not to impede the Jewish Agency program.

Mr. Schind reported that he had given instructions for the Milca to proceed from Bulgaria to Constanza, and that/additional boat, the Salah-Aladin, is likewise in Constanza. Practically, under present circumstances, it does not seem likely that any Turkish boats will be able to leave Istanbul for Constanza.

In summing up the discussion of evacuation of Jewish people from Budapest, via the Danube, it was understood for the time being that the Jewish Agency is making a thorough investigation of the situation and transport possibilities, and that for the time being the War Refugee Board would not authorize Mr. Jabotinsky to send a man to Hungary for this purpose.

VI. Mr. Barlas reported the following matters: (a) He had received a cable from Mr. Zissu to the effect that lists of pass-engers for the Smyrnie have been prepared and submitted to the proper channels; (b) In a telegram from Mr. Zissu he was informed that the Rumanian government had agreed to provide transit visas to Jewish people in Hungary requiring Rumanian transit facilities, and the necessary instructions have been officially sent to the

Rumanian consulate in Budapest; (c) He had spoken with the British Embassy in Ankara about a proposal to send Turkish rolling stock to Budapest for the transportation by railroad of evacuees from Hungary, and the British Embassy had promised to send an appropriate note on the subject to the Turkish Foreign Office. In this connection, the War Refugee Board might be requested to give guarantees to the Turkish authorities to protect them against the loss or non-return of the Turkish carriages. However, this project is immature and should be held over for consideration until next week.

There being no further business, the meeting adjourned.

MINUTES

of a Meeting
of the Operating Group of Relief Organizations
at the Office of the War Refugee Board, Istanbul
August 21, 1944, 4:45 p.m.

Those present: I. A. Hirschmann, Herbert Katzki, Reuben
Resnik, Charles Passman, Zeev Schind, Ehud Ueberall, Chaim
Barlas.

Prior to the meeting, Mr. Schweitzer telephoned to say
that because of other engagements which he had made and which
he was not able to cancel, he could not be present.

Mr. Hirschmann opened the meeting by requesting information concerning the investigation of the Mefkura sinking.
He reported that the United States Naval Attache's office
was not able to make anyone available to attend the examination which would be made of the respective captains of the
Mefkura and the Bülbül. He reported, however, that the
British Naval Attache agreed to make available to him a copy
of their report when it has been prepared.

Mr. Barlas stated that the examination of the two captains
was expected to take place within the next few days. Such
examination should not be made solely from the technical
point of view, which might be that of the Naval Attache, but
from the point of view of the rescue organizations, in order
to determine the feasibility of continued rescue work by sea.
He stated that he had cabled to Mr. Zissu in Bucharest requesting the
names of the passengers on the Mefkura. His own view was
that because of the last-minute redistribution of the passengers among the three boats, such lists might not be available
in Rumania. He himself is sending to Bucharest the names of
the Bülbül and Morina passengers, so that through a process
of elimination the names of those on the Mefkura might be
determined.

Inquiry had been made by members of the Istanbul Jewish
community regarding reports that 130 bodies had been washed

ashore along the Black Sea coast. It appears that this report is not true.

Although Mr. Simond of the International Red Cross seems to question the report that the Mefkura was sunk by gun-fire, discussions with the five surviving passengers definitely indicate that this is true.

Mr. Schind stated that one of the British naval officers said that he would make an assistant available to talk to the captains of the Bülbül and the Mefkura.

Mr. Hirschmann introduced the subject of the telegram received by Mr. Simond from the International Red Cross delegate, Kolb, in Bucharest, by reading the telegram of August 16 to the meeting (copy attached to these minutes), with reference to the status of Mr. Zissu in emigration work and the proposed sailing of the Alba Julia. Simond wanted to reply on the preceding Friday or Saturday, August 18 or 19, but he had dissuaded him from doing so until the matter could be discussed among the representatives of the relief organizations. Mr. Barlas reported that he had cabled Zissu confirming that he was the representative of the Jewish Agency and that he has plein pouvoir to do whatever is necessary with regard to the Rubin situation. He thinks that Zissu required a strengthening of his position in his relationships with the Government and that he is quite capable of handling the Rubin matter. He had advised Mr. Simond to inform Kolb to the effect that Zissu is the representative of the Jewish Agency in emigration matters. Mr. Schind explained the status of the Orat for the benefit of Mr. Passman. In his view, if Zissu is to represent the Jewish Agency, Barlas should instruct him specifically as to what to do and that he should not be given entire discretion, but he should be informed that the Orat is not to be eliminated until another organization has been established through which ships can be sent. It is this function, namely, which Orat now serves. Mr. Barlas stated that he is sending a second cable to Zissu ordering the prompt dispatch of the ships now in Constanza. He agreed to make copies of both wires available to Mr. Hirschmann.

Mr. Resnik stated that the JDC had received complaints about the Orat, but nevertheless had advised Mr. Fildermann that the Orat should go ahead with its work. However, if complaints continue, and the flow of people is impeded because of the differences in leadership, the question should be reviewed.

Mr. Passman reported that upon the eve of his departure from Palestine to Istanbul wires were received by Mr. Kaplan from Zissu via Switzerland to the effect that if Zissu is not given full control of emigration work, the flow of refugees will stop.

Mr. Schind was of the opinion that if Mr. Zissu represents the Jewish Agency, and is doing his work properly, he is obliged to work with the Orat and to make every effort to send to Istanbul those ships which are now ready and available in Constanza. Mr. Zissu apparently desires to eliminate the Orat.

Mr. Hirschmann emphasized that internal questions involving the status of various Jewish Agency people or their respective organizations is not on in which he can interfere, but that the interests of the War Refugee Board can only arise if such disputes result in a blocking of emigration work. He asked that these differences be composed outside the meeting, and the final steps taken be reported at the next meeting.

Mr. Barlas analyzed the telegrams he had received from Zissu concerning the proposed voyage of the Alba Julia. The proposals were based upon the transportation of 4000 passengers. This would cost, according to the proposals, two hundred million lei, plus 20 million lei for insurance of the equipage, plus 30 million lei for other internal costs. This would aggregate 56,000 lei per person, or 13 pounds. The insurance of the boat would cost additionally 12 pounds per person. If the number of passengers were reduced to 3,000, the costs per passengers would be 17 pounds plus 12 pounds.

It was proposed that five million Swiss francs be deposited as an insurance guarantee for the value of the vessel, in the event that it is lost, or alternatively that insurance be purchased with insurance companies. According to Mr. Barlas, the premium rate would be 12 per cent. According to the telegram, it would be possible for the Alba Julia to leave within ten days, if financing details and necessary authorizations could be given immediately.

Mr. Hirschmann was of the opinion that this question of financing ought to be determined by the Jewish Agency and the JDC together, and suggested that this be done subject to report at the next meeting.

Mr. Schind reported that the Salahaldin and Smyrnie are in Constanza, and the Milca will be departing shortly from Varna to Constanza. In addition, it is contemplated that two additional boats be sent from Istanbul for the embarkation of refugees in Rumania. Mr.Hirschmann emphasized the importance of moving the people from Rumania at the earliest possible moment, so that the way would be clear for the refugees from Hungary in the event that the several proposed projects be realized. Although he will propose that the

-5-

Hungarian refugees be permitted to remain in Rumania until their onward voyage is possible, it will be necessary for the good of the work in general to move them promptly. Under such circumstances the way would be cleared and boats available.

Mr. Hirschmann read a memorandum dated August 14 concerning railroad transportation from Bulgaria. He reported that according to this memorandum, movement from Bulgaria may take place via railroad should it become apparent that the _Vita_ and the _Pirin_ are unable to engage in a shuttle service between Burgas and Istanbul.

Mr. Barlas reported that he had received telegrams to the effect that 140 children were ready to come from Rumania but that the Turkish Consul had refused the necessary visas, interpreting his instructions as meaning that he is permitted to grant visas only for sea travel. This matter has now been clarified.

Mr. Barlas reported further that he had sent 1,000 Palestine certificate confirmations to Bulgaria, to be used as a basis for Turkish transit visa applications for overland travel, and that both Bucharest and Budapest had been advised of the general overall agreement concerning Turkish transit visas which had been made by the Turkish Foreign Office.

Mr. Schind had received a cable that Bulgarian authorities would not permit the _Vita_ and _Pirin_ to leave Bulgaria because of the _Mefkura_ disaster. A recent arrival from Bulgaria brought a message from Joseph Levy of the Russe community saying that the passengers are ready for the _Pirin_ and he thinks that they will be able to depart shortly. In his opinion, people in Bulgaria are still prepared to leave that country, despite reported prospects that the condition of Jewish people in that country will be ameliorated.

Mr. Hirschmann advised the meeting that the order on the part of the Bulgarians which had been holding up the departure of the _Vita_ and _Pirin_ has been cancelled.

Mr. Hirschmann reported briefly on the political situation in Bulgaria, insofar as the Jewish people there are concerned. He had let it be known to the Bulgarian authorities that as far as the United States Government is concerned they desire that emigration from Bulgaria take place on a voluntary basis, and that it should not be a forced emigration, because of the failure on the part of the Bulgarian authorities to eliminate the anti-Jewish laws. In his opinion, the number of people who will want to emigrate from Bulgaria will be substantially reduced, should representations concerning the elimination of the anti-Jewish laws be carried out. Quite possibly, however, the young people may still want to emigrate. In the meanwhile, the United States Government has requested Ambassador Harriman in Moscow to make such representations as might be feasible to enlist the support of the Russian Government in persuading the Bulgarians to take ameliorating steps in its relationships towards the Jews.

Mr. Barlas suggested that since the Allied Governments had criticized the actions of the satellite countries in oppressing the Jews, and had broadcast warnings to them, they ought now to approve the action taken by the Bulgarian Government, should it change its policy in that connection. In this connection Mr. Hirschmann indicated that the War Refugee Board had already been informed of the advisability of doing just that thing.

-7-

Mr. Barlas stated that he had received a telegram to the effect that 2195 persons are ready to leave Hungary and are in possession of Hungarian exit and Rumanian transit visas, but that German consent for the departure of these people is still required. The organizations in Hungary are pursuing this matter further.

Mr. Passman presented the offer made by Palestinian transportation companies to make available 400 lorries for transporting refugees. This was discussed in the meeting, and the general impression was that complexities arising out of the shortage of gasoline, the necessity for crossing military zones, travelling through Axis countries, might make such a proposal unfeasible. It was decided that this offer should be investigated further as to its practicability.

Mr. Schind, who expected to be departing for Palestine on August 24, took occasion to express his thanks for the assistance and cooperation which he had received from the War Refugee Board in connection with that part of the transportation of refugees in which he and his associates are interested. He expressed the hope that the War Refugee Board would continue its friendly efforts in collaboration with his associates who will remain in Istanbul to carry on the work.

Mr. Hirschmann, in acknowledging Mr. Schind's request, assured him of the continuing assistance of the War Refugee Board and asked him to tell his colleagues in Palestine that despite all obstacles the agencies in Istanbul were working harder than before.

There being no further business, the meeting was adjourned at 6:15 p.m.

Herbert Katzki

Telegram attached

Attachment to Minutes

## TELEGRAMME REÇU DE KOLB, le 16 AOUT

Les correspondants des institutions juives, qui ont ma confiance, m'ont montré le télégramme qu'ils ont adressé à Istanbul, et me demandent de l'appuyer énergiquement.

Je vous prie de vouloir bien faire comprendre à Istanbul, que l'ORAT doit être définitivement écarté, et que RUBIN, contre lequel existent des griefs sérieux, doit être congédié; sans de telles mesures, l'émigration juive sera gravement compromise.

La question doit être entre les mains de M. ZISSU, qui est un homme intègre et appuyé par le Gouvernement Roumain. Ceci d'autant que l'on prévoit le prochain passage d'un grand nombre d'émigrés hongrois.

L'affrètement du bateau ALBAJULIA se prépare et sera utilisé pour l'émigration jusqu'à Istanbul. La capacité de transport est de quatre mille personnes.

La question de l'achat des deux bateaux roumains stationnés dans le port d'Istanbul est de nouveau à l'ordre du jour. Veuillez me câbler d'urgence si M. Hirschman ou autre organisme juif peuvent garantir une somme de 5 millions (?) pour le voyage aller et retour de l'ALBAJULIA.

Votre message 666 ne m'est parvenu que ce jour. ORAT est responsable du nombre des passagers ayant pris place sur les bateaux qui furent envoyés par ses soins.

Je suis dans l'attente de vos renseignements au sujet du naufrage du MEFKURE.

Kolb

# MINUTES

of a Meeting
of the Operating Group of Relief Organizations
in the Office of Mr. Barlas, August 17, 1944, 7:00 p.m.

Those present: I. A. Hirschmann, Herbert Katzki, Zeev Schind,
Reuben Resnik, David Schweitzer, Chaim Barlas.

Mr. Hirschmann opened the meeting by suggesting that it would be advisable at this time to review the projects for evacuating refugees from Rumania by sea, in view of the Mefkura disaster. In this connection, he alluded to WRB cable No. 97. Mr. Barlas reported that a small committee, consisting of Messrs. Barlas, Resnik, and Meyerhoff, is investigating all the facts, as far as they can be ascertained, regarding the sinking, and that a full report will be made upon the conclusion of their investigations. In the meanwhile, it is his opinion that evacuation by sea from Rumania must contine, and he has already written Mr. Zissu to that effect.

Mr. Resnik stated that the Mefkura survivors and the Bülbül passengers with whom he spoke felt that the dangers of sea transportation were pretty strong, and that something more ought to be done in terms of safety if movement by sea is to continue. If Rumanian naval escorts of the boats up to Bulgarian waters could be secured, why could not similar safety measures be taken for the voyage beyond that point? Telegrams which he had seen and which were being sent to Rumania to relatives in Rumania by Bülbül passengers advised against leaving Constanza by boat for the voyage to Istanbul.

Mr. Schind pointed out that investigations of the disaster are not yet complete. Information thus far to hand was that the Mefkura travelled without lights and that warnings from the attacking boats that the Mefkura stop its engines and stand by were disregarded. It is important to know whether similar signals to stop were received by the Bülbül and exactly what the circumstances were under which it did stop and subsequently continue its voyage.

The three refugee boats were escorted by Rumanian vessels and sailed under German permission, under specific instructions as to route. These are factors which have a bearing upon the investigation. The insurance companies are also checking up on the facts.

Mr. Barlas suggested that an effort be made to secure the assistance of members of the American and British Attaches offices in conducting the inquiry. Mr. Schind was of the opinion that until the investigation was finished there should be no change in policy regarding movement by ship. Perhaps people in Rumania will be unwilling to travel by sea, but this would be their decision and not ours. It is only by moving people from Rumania that it will be possible to assist refugees from Hungary who will be dependent upon Rumanian transit facilities. It should be noted that the Mefkura was the first ship which was a casualty after eight others had successfully completed their trips to Istanbul. Mr. Schweitzer felt that people in Rumania are in possession of all the facts, and they will decide as to whether or not they wish to travel by sea. In the meanwhile, they must be given the opportunity to make their own decision in this regard.

Mr. Hirschmann summarized the position by stating that it was agreed by all present in principle as to the need for continuing sea transportation. However, this leads to several questions: first, what safety provisions can be taken for future voyages; secondly, for whom shall the ships be made available, for Rumanians, Bulgarians, or Hungarians; and thirdly, what delayed the departure of the Morina, Bülbül and Mefkura.

Mr. Schind stated that it was impossible to answer the last question definitely, but it was the opinion of his group in the absence of other information that the delay was the result of internal politics. He can only hope that, because of various steps which have been taken, such discord will not arise in the future. Zissu, Fildermann, and Petrusca all were involved in the dissensions. Some of the delays may have occurred because of the methods of financing transportation, which involved the choosing of people who are in a position to pay sufficient sums for their passages to cover internal expenditures which must be made in Rumania.

If the Bellacita or other Bulgarian boat can be sent at once to Constanza, this should be done. This will have a good moral effect even if it must sail with a small number of people. Indeed, orders have already been dispatched to Constanza that the Salahaldin be sent off, carrying any number of persons, however small, who are willing to make the trip at this time. In a cable from Bucharest, dated August 14, Mr. Schind's group was advised that arrangements for the rebuilding of the Salahaldin are going on, and it will be ready to make the trip within the next few days. With the Smyrnie, likewise, preparations for accomodating passengers are going forward. In his opinion, the work must go on because at this moment there is no other solution to the transportation question.

Mr. Resnik was of the opinion that up to the present time there was no factor in the situation which should cause the stoppage of sea transport. However, maximum efforts for safety must be taken. Some survivors reported to him that life-saving equipment was not satisfactory. They were sufficient in number, but deficient in quality. There were language difficulties, inasmuch as none of the passengers

-4-

could speak Turkish, and neither the captain nor the crew members knew any other language. Means of egress from the boat were likewise inadequate.

According to Mr. Schweitzer, the version of some of the people was that it was impossible for the Mefkura passengers below decks to get out of the hold. In his opinion, clarification should likewise be secured of a current report that 15 per cent of the passengers must pay for the voyage in order to cover internal expenses, or the departure of boats is delayed.

Mr. Barlas stated that any refugee can leave Rumania without paying transportation, and that up to the present time no refugee has been required to pay for his voyage.

Mr. Hirschmann thought it advisable to withhold judgment until the full report of the investigating committee be received, but that in the meanwhile all efforts for sea transport should continue. The possibilities that escorts be sent with the boats who are able to interpret languages should likewise be checked. Mr. Schind stated that orders have been sent to Constanza that better life-belts must be found, that all passengers must wear their life-belts at all times, that not more than one ship should be en route at any one time, that people able to act as interpreters be provided for the ships, and that the number of persons embarked on the vessels should be reduced in order to avoid over-crowding. In this connection, instructions have already been sent to Bucharest to embark no more than 400 passengers on the Salahaldin, on which it was originally planned to send 600.

Mr. Hirschmann ████████ introduced for discussion the manner in which the Bülbül passengers were received and sheltered in Istanbul. He stated that according to reports received by him, there was substantial room for improvement

in the matter of organization. Mr. Barlas thought that the
refugees were satisfied and that everything went all right.
It must be taken into account that the local people who
assisted in the work at the Jewish school where the people
were sheltered were without experience in the matter. Mr.
Resnik pointed out that the school facilities were not set
up for the kind of service which was expected of them, and
that in his opinion the matter was handled satisfactorily.

Mr. Schweitzer stated that on the whole the work was
done satisfactorily, but was of the opinion that there was
substantial room for improvement in terms of the organization
of the work in providing medical assistance and other types
of aid. Although the dining-room was well organized, there
was substantial room for improvement in other aspects of
the work.

Mr. Hirschmann, to sum up, felt that it was important
that the representatives of the other organizations in Istanbul
many of whom have had experience in the movement of refugees
ought to be given some responsibility where emergencies of
the present kind arose, all in the interest of the task to
be performed.

Mr. Hirschmann requested information regarding the status
of the SS _Vita_ and _Pirin_. Mr. Schind reported that he had
sent orders to Burgas to prepare these boats for departure
but was without reply. Mr. Barlas' experience in communica-
ting with the official Jewish Agency representative in
Bulgaria likewise remained without response. The reason for
the absence of replies is not known. Perhaps Bulgarian
Jewish people, because of the _Mefkura_ disaster, were
unwilling to take the risk of the sea voyage, as perhaps
they did not feel the urgent pressure to leave as did xxx

-6-

for example the refugees who had entered Rumania. In any
event, this matter is being followed up closely, and if no
response is received within the next three or four days,
other steps will be taken.

Mr. Barlas then read to the meeting a letter dated
August 12, 1944, which he had received from the British
Embassy in Ankara, summarizing the terms of an agreement
which had been made by the Turkish Foreign Office with reference to the issuance of Turkish transit visas to applicants
therefor in Hungary, Rumania and Bulgaria, and who were in
possession of certain documents as a basis for supporting
their requests.

In the above connection, Mr. Hirschmann read in full
the entire text of the telegram which was sent by the British
Embassy in Ankara to the Foreign Office, London, and which
gave in detail the terms of the agreement. He reported that
he had asked Mr. Simond of the International Red Cross to
inform Intercross delegates in Hungary, Rumania and Bulgaria
of the Turkish transit visa facilities now made possible
under the agreement.

Mr. Barlas reported that he had sent a test group of
100 confirmations to the Jewish Agency representative in
Bulgaria, to determine whether or not it will be possible
for the holders thereof to cross the Turkish border without
further ado, as a test of the possibilities under the
agreement. Instructions had been dispatched by cable and
letter to Budapest to sent a first group of 600 refugees to
Rumania or Bulgaria as a further test.

Discussion then ensued as to the manner in which people
from Hungary can be transported, with particular reference
to rail traffic difficulties. It was pointed out that, under

-7-

the agreement, apparently movement from the satellite countries was to be confined to sea voyages, on the **Pirin** and
**Vita**, and that on these grounds rail entry into Turkey was
to cease.

Mr. Barlas reported that this part of the agreement has
since been amended, and that land traffic is to be kept open.
The British Embassy agreed to sent a special memorandum to
the Foreign Office on the subject.

Mr. Barlas reported further that he had a message from
Switzerland that two groups of children should be leaving
shortly from Bulgaria. He expected to investigate this
matter further in Ankara within the next few days.

With regard to Hungary, Mr. Barlas reported that word
had been received from Kraus and Komly, a Jewish Agency leader
in Budapest, by letter, which left ten days ago, which
indicated that, first: Kraus is optimistic as to possibilities
for emigration from Hungary; second: Komly reports that
although the Hungarians agreed in principle, they have taken
no steps to put these principles into action.

Mr. Barlas has received definite information that Rumanian
transit visas for Hungarian refugees have been arranged, but
has no information up to the present time regarding Bulgarian
transit. He thought it advisable that steps be taken to
secure free passage through Bulgaria in behalf of Hungarian
Jews. Should this facility be secured, it would then be
possible to bring further pressure in Hungary for release of
refugees from that country.

There being no further business, the meeting was
adjourned at 8:30.

Herbert Katzki

August 15, 1944

Notes for use at 7:00 p.m. conference

1. Ship program:

   (a) Rumania;

   (b) Review of Mefkura,
       handling of people in school and train;

   (c) Reasons learned now for delay;

   (d) Future program.

2. Bulgaria:

   (a) Perin and Vita; ✓

   (b) Kelley's talk with British Foreign Office;

   (c) Children from Bulgaria due to arrive August 10.

3. Hungary:

   (a) Where does rescue work stand? British Foreign Off. memo;

   (b) Talk at Consulate;

   (c) Movement across borders;

4. British Foreign Office memo.

MINUTES

of a meeting
of Representatives of Relief Organizations
at the office of the War Refugee Board
Istanbul, August 25, 1944

Those present: I. A. Hirschmann, Herbert Katzki, Irving H.
Sherman, for the War Refugee Board; Reuben Resnik, Charles
Passman, Mordecai Kessler, for the Joint Distribution Com-
mittee; Chaim Barlas, J. Golden, Saul Meyerhoff, Moshe
Averbuch, Ehud Ueberall, Mnachim Bader, Venja Pomeraniec,
for the Jewish Agency; Leon Denenberg, for the International
Rescue and Relief Committee; Eri Jabotinsky, for the Emer-
gency Committee for the Rescue of Jewish People in Europe;
David Schweitzer, for the Hias-Ica Emigration Association
(Hicem); Jacob Griffel, Joseph Klarman, and Ludwig Kastner
for the Agudath Israel and the Vaad Hahatzalah.

David Zymand of the Jewish Agency was present by invi-
tation. Akiba Levinsky and Eliezer Leder were unable to be
present, and sent their excuses.

The meeting was called to order at 4:15 by Mr. Hirschmann, as chairman.

Mr. Hirschmann opened the meeting by welcoming Messrs.
Passman, Kessler, Meyerhoff, Ueberall, Pomeraniec, and Sherman, who had arrived in Istanbul subsequent to the previous
meeting of representatives of relief organizations, July 10.
He expressed his regrets at the departure of Mr. Schind, who
had left Istanbul for Palestine.

Mr. Hirschmann reviewed briefly the activities of the
War Refugee Board representatives in Istanbul subsequent to
July 10, and the rescue work which had been accomplished by
the various agencies since that date, under the following
headings:

(a) Efforts made to ameliorate the status of Jewish
people in Bulgaria by means of the abrogation of the Bulgarian
anti-Jewish laws.

(b) Steps taken to secure the consent of the Rumanian
Government to the departure of Jewish people from that country, the granting of transit facilities by the Rumanian Government to Jewish people fleeing from Hungary, and the shel-
tering of Hungarian Jews in Rumania pending the preparation
of transportation facilities for their further travel to

Istanbul and Palestine.

(c) Negotiations and discussions with the Turkish authorities culminating in the broad agreement on the part of the Turkish Foreign Office concerning the issuance of Turkish transit visas in Hungary, Rumania, and Bulgaria, and the entry into Turkey in transit of refugees traveling by land and by sea.

(d) The present situation in Hungary in consequence of the promulgation of July 18, 1944, by the Hungary Government, with reference to the emigration of Jewish people from Hungary in certain categories and under certain conditions.

(e) Transports which have passed through Istanbul on the SS Kazbek, Morina, Bülbül, and overland.

(f) Projects which had been submitted to the War Refugee Board representatives for consideration, notably by Mr. Griffel for emigration from Rumania, and by Mr. Jabotinsky for emigration from Budapest via the Danube.

Mr. Hirschmann referred also to projects of emigration which are in varying stages of completion, namely the voyages of the SS Smyrnie, Salahaldin, Alba Julia, and perhaps the Milca, from Constanza, and the SS Vita and Pirin, from Burgas. Analysis was made also of the possible effect upon emigration and rescue work by the changing attitude of Bulgaria regarding Jewish people in its territory, and the recent defection of the Rumanian Government from its German alliances to the Allied side.

In explaining the present policy of the War Refugee Board, Mr. Hirschmann stated that, although fundamental changes in Bulgaria seem to be under consideration, and the United Nations may shortly be in control in Rumania, nevertheless efforts will continue to evacuate Jewish people and

-2-

others from both those countries so long as it appears that their lives are in danger because of racial, religious, or political beliefs. Although present information is to the effect that the German authorities in Budapest have not sanctioned the departure of Jewish people from Hungary, despite the public pronouncement of Admiral Horthy, efforts for their evacuation will continue in any manner and in any direction which seem feasible.

During the discussion which followed Mr. Hirschmann's review, Mr. Ueberall made the following observations:

(1) It must not be assumed that it is either too late or that too short a time remains for the evacuation of people from Rumania, but every effort must be made to take advantage of whatever opportunities exist for evacuating people from Rumania before emigration becomes impossible, should the United Nations in control in that country deem it advisable to restrict emigration.

(2) While no information is available regarding the situation on the Hungarian-Rumanian border, one must assume that penetration of refugees from Hungary to Rumania will cease, as a result of which it will be necessary to find other areas to which Jewish people can be sent: either to Switzerland or via Jugoslavia to other countries. He suggested, therefore, that the War Refugee Board address itself to these two possibilities.

Mr. Hirschmann informed the meeting of the efforts long since initiated by the War Refugee Board through its representatives in Switzerland, Sweden, Portugal, North Africa, Italy, and elsewhere to assist not only the refugees from Hungary but from other countries. He also pointed out the importance of keeping the War Refugee Board representatives in Istanbul currently informed of all information which might come into the possession of the representatives of the relief organizations here, and which might have a bearing upon or would provide fresh points of view in the development of rescue and relief work programs.

Mr. Barlas re-emphasized the need for continuing rescue work at full pressure and stated that he had already instructed the Jewish Agency representatives in the various countries of emigration to continue their efforts to the maximum. He thought it important that despite possible amelioration in Rumania and Bulgaria the situation must be closely observed, and that, in addition, full attention must be directed upon the problem of Hungary.

Mr. Sherman stated that all work must continue as though no changes had occurred. Should the situation improve, the only loss will be one of energy which will have been expended in following various projects. If the situation does not improve, no time will have been lost.

Mr. Barlas advised the meeting that several group of children traveling overland from Rumania and Bulgaria are expected and that in addition 1050 Jewish Agency certificate confirmations have been sent through the Bulgarian Embassy to the Jewish Agency representative in Bulgaria, as a basis for requesting Turkish transit visas in accordance with the agreement of the Turkish Foreign Office.

A general discussion ensued on various matters which had been reported at the meeting.

There being no further formal business, the meeting was adjourned at 5:30.

Herbert Katzki

72

NOTES:

Welcome and introduce newcomers. -- Messrs.
Passman, Kessler, Meyeroff, Ueberall,
Pomeraniec and Sherman (pro tem.) Mention
Shind has left.

1. Review of events that happened since last meeting:

    (a) Efforts politically

        (1) Attempts to bring pressure upon Bulgarians
            to take fundamental steps regarding the
            Jewish citizenry. (This problem is still
            in process).

        (2) Efforts to have Rumanians permit Jews to
            ~~go into Hungary.~~ *travel facilities to Hungary and*
            *Israeli travel facilities to Hungary*

        (3) Relationship with Turkish people on
            transit visas, travel, etc. New code
            (Exhibit A) for Hungary, July 18 decree.
            Inability of Germans to permit Jews to
            leave.

    (b) After last meeting we left for the Kazbek
        since then there arrived the two other boats, —
        and the sinking of the Mefkura about which
        we have the final report. Read this report.
        (Exhibit B)

        (1) Group of 43 children from Bulgaria.

        (2) Decision to keep up our rescue work in this
            field. (Exhibit C - Telegram No. 694)

    (c) Numbers of projects of various kinds that have
        been submitted:

        (1) Griffel

        (2) Danube boats (Jabotinsky)

2. Changing scene:

    (a) Bulgaria and Jewish question

    (b) Rumanian defection

    (c) War scare in Turkey.

    (d)

3. Present status of projects:

    (a) Smyrnie, Salahaldin, and perhaps Milka, Constanza,
        and Alba Julia from Rumania. Information
        received today from Kolb that the Salahaldin
        is about to leave with 1,000 passengers.

    (b) Vita and Perin from Bulgaria

    (c) Movement from Hungary

73

4. Open meeting for new suggestions.

5. Position of the Board that we are proceeding in our program of rescue without cessation until we have information that the situation does not require it.

   (a) The condition in Hungary is as bad or worse then it was before.

   (b) Bulgaria is a belligerent and the situation there requires attention until political moves indicate otherwise. We have managed to include the Jewish question as a major issue in the platform of the Bagryanov Government's apparent desire to withdraw from the war.

   (c) Rumania is still an open question. If it becomes a battle ground similar to Italy, as indicated by Cretzianu that it will, we may have very serious problems of rescue. Our decision is to watch and wait and to function.

22.8.44

1. Further interrogation of the captains of MEFKURE and BÜLBÜL took place today.

2. All evidence shows that MEFKURE was sunk on August 5th about 0130 localtime,about 25 miles N. E. of IGNEADA, by gunfire from one of two (or possibly three) submarines on the surface. The gun used was probably a 20 m/m automatic cannon with explosive missile.

3. It is evident that the skipper of the MEFKURE lost his head and abandoned ship at the first hit; his statement that he received no warning is therefore discounted in view of the statements of

    (a) the captain of the BÜLBÜL (a steady witness) that he saw a red rocket fired on his starboard bow at about 2230/4th at approximately the point where MEFKURE was at the time.

    (b) other survivors of the MEFKURE who state that the enemy vessel made lamp signals in the direction of the ship, and fired a red rocket.

4. According to the captain of the MEFKURE the attacking vessel came up from astern, firing as she came, passed by the stationary vessel to starboard, still firing, and crossed ahead of her. Fire was then opened on the dinghy, in which were the captain and crew of the vessel. They promptly jumped out, and the dinghy was hit three times and smashed.

Paraphrase of Telegram Received from
Washington as No. 694, August 10, 5 PM

- - - - - - - - - -

Hirschmann is sent the following telegram (WRB Cable No. 97) from the War Refugee Board. The following is in reference to the Embassy's telegrams Nos. 1445 of August 7, 1429 of August 5 and 1437 of August 7. The sinking of the refugee ship MEFKURA* with the loss of lives which resulted is regretted by the Board, though the safe arrival of the ships MARINA and BULBUL is very encouraging. The Board greatly appreciates the efforts of Hirschmann and Kelley in connection with the above.

Any information in addition to that which has already been furnished concerning the sinking of the MEFKURA will be appreciated by the War Refugee Board, though it is appreciated that security requirements may prevent the sending of certain details.

With reference to the Embassy's telegram No. 1445, the War Refugee Board will fully support the decision which you make with respect to possible future voyages of the Bulgarian or any other boats indicated in the telegram under reference, after you have consulted with the private organizations involved and with the Embassy. The Board knows that the decision which you will reach will take into account the comparative risks to the refugees of the uncertainties of sea voyages or the perils of remaining in Hungary, Rumania or Bulgaria, as the case may be. It is assumed that the refugees themselves have been warned, through the appropriate private organizations, of the risks which such voyages involve. The JDC has been informed of the above and agrees with the statements above.

* (Code letters missing, but words supplied by Code Room)

MINUTES

of a Meeting
of the Operating Group of Relief Organizations
at the Office of the War Refugee Board, Istanbul
September 4, 1944.

Those present: I. A. Hirschmann, Chairman; Herbert Katzki,
Chaim Barlas, Dr. Eliash, Charles Passman, Mordecai Kessler,
David Schweitzer, Enud Ueberall.

The meeting was called to order at 4:30 p.m.

I. Mr. Barlas reported the following:

A. His trip to Ankara on August 29 was in connection with routine affairs of the Jewish Agency, especially
regarding the emigration to Palestine of 300 children in
Rumania and Bulgaria, whose Turkish transit visas had expired.
These transit visas are being renewed.

B. A recent telegram from Bulgaria reports that
the SS Vita, one of the ships which was to be used to carry
emigrants from Bulgaria to Istanbul, had been sunk. Steps
are now being taken to replace this ship in accordance with
agreements previously made.

C. Several discussions have been had with Mr.
Bratiano from Bucharest concerning emigration from Rumania.
The picture Bratiano drew indicated that the emigration situa-
tion in Bucharest was complicated, as a result of which Mr.
Barlas has decided to go to Bucharest. Mr. Cretzianu, the
Rumanian Minister to Turkey, has given his consent, provided
the British agree. The British have cabled to London for
instructions.

D. He referred Mr. Bratiano to Mr. Passman on
questions relating to relief for Jewish people in Rumania.

E. Concerning the reported obstructionist tactics
of Mr. Zissu, which are said to have resulted in a reduction
of thousands in the numbers of persons evacuated from Rumania
by sea, Mr. Zissu had been recommended for appointment as
Jewish Agency representative in Rumania by all Zionist

-2-

organizations in that country. Mr. Bratiano told a one-sided story, and decision should be reserved regarding Mr. Zissu until he has opportunity for reporting his version of events.

Referring to point E above, Mr. Hirschmann reported that Mr. Passman, Mr. Katzki and he had had a long conference with Mr. Bratiano, who described in some detail the clash of personalities which had taken place in Bucharest and which, he said, had been the result in substantial measure of the autocratic and arbitrary actions of Mr. Zissu. Mr. Hirschmann stated that the War Refugee Board will not condone any such attitudes, and that it will refuse its aid, financially or in any other way, to projects which reflect personality clashes, partisanship and rivalry to the detriment of the objective of rescue activities, and are not democratic in their conception and execution.

II. Discussion was had regarding the policy to be followed for rescue work from Rumania in the future.

A. Mr. Hirschmann referred to the terms of reference of the War Refugee Board, which limited its activities to the rescue of persons who, for reasons of race, religion, or political beliefs, were in imminent peril of death, and which excluded the normal emigration of people who desire to go to another country. Under such circumstances, the Board's program in Rumania might have to be limited to the assistance of refugees, should investigation make it apparent that the general situation of Rumanian Jews in that country has been ameliorated. Furthermore, the War Refugee Board could not be used as an instrument to assist in the immigration of people into Palestine in response to a desire on the part of the Jewish Agency to build up that country, for reasons of its own.

B. Mr. Barlas stated that if investigations indicate that non-Rumanian nationals in Rumania must be evacuated, they

-3-

will all, without exception and without discrimination, be given Palestine certificates. To this end, refugees will have priority in whatever emigration movement from Rumania takes place.

C. Dr. Eliash formulated the Jewish Agency position as follows:

"Unless some general statement is made by the Rumanian Government in behalf of refugees in that country, and the children from Transnistria, they will be regarded as the first charge upon the emigration work of the Jewish Agency. Otherwise, their emigration as well as that of Rumanian nationals will be regarded as normal and voluntary."

D. Mr. Passman stated that the Joint Distribution Committee will not finance the movement of ships from Rumania or anywhere else unless the Joint Distribution Committee has a measure of control in such projects. Rescue work will be conducted jointly by representatives of the War Refugee Board, the Joint Distribution Committee, and the Jewish Agency. Normal emigration work will be in the hands of the Jewish Agency.

III. Mr. Hirschmann reported that the color of the new Bulgarian Government indicated that it may be expected to carry out the policy initiated by the Bagryanov Government, with reference to the withdrawal of the Bulgarian anti-Jewish laws. Although the War Refugee Board is prepared to continue to their conclusion such projects which it had previously approved for the evacuation of Jewish people from Bulgaria and other countries, the improvement in the situation of the Jews in Bulgaria removes this country from among those whose minority groups are of interest to the War Refugee Board for purposes of evacuation. The War Refugee Board is now considering the manner in which assistance might be given to the Joint Distribution Committee to enable the latter to introduce a program

-4-

of temporary and emergency relief for the Jewish people in
Bulgaria.

IV. Mr. Hirschmann made reference to reports which have
been received in Istanbul indicating that the Jewish Agency
representative in Budapest, Kraus, had taken certain steps
which served to block the mechanism which had been established
for moving Hungarian Jews to Rumania. Mr. Barlas stated that
the circumstances were such that Kraus had no alternative,
unless he was prepared to have a number of individuals
engaged in rescue work for profit take over the work of the
Jewish Agency in Hungary.

There being no further business, the meeting was adjourned
at 5:45 p.m.

Herbert Katzki

9/4/44

Notes fo Use at the Meeting, September 4

1. Barlas' talk with Cr.

Also, the results of his conferences in Ankara during
the course of his last trip there.

2. Ask Barlas about the contract which he has with Antalya.
He has never reported this in any of the meetings.

3. What does the Jewish Agency propose doing about the
situation in Rumania as reported by Bratiano, especially with
regard to the reported obstructionist tactics of Mr. Zissu
and his group.

4. What does the Jewish Agency propose doing about the
situation in Hungary, as reported by Mr. Janos, who told about
discrimination in the issuance of certificates, Kraus' fighting
in the office of the Rumanian Consulate, which resulted in the
break-down of the procedure which had been worked out for
bringing people from Hungary to Rumania.

5. Proposed policy of the WRB in connection with rescue
activities from the Balkan countries.

a. Bulgaria, in view of the anti-Jewish laws, probably
does not warrant a rescue program but only normal emigration.

b. Rumania—the Rumanian nationals themselves perhaps
may be able to remain in that country, leaving open only the
question of the evacuation of non-Rumanian nationals in that
country. What to do about this remains to be seen. In the
meanwhile, such normal emigration as there may be from any of
these countries the WRB proposes to regard as a normal business
flowing through the hands of the JDC, in cooperation with such
representation of the Jewish Agency as may be decided upon
among themselves.

M I N U T E S

of a meeting
of the Co-operating Group of Relief Organizations
at the office of the War Refugee Board, Istanbul
September 22, 1944

Those present: I. A. Hirschmann, Herbert Katzki, for the War
Refugee Board; M. Bader; J. Golden, for the Jewish Agency;
C. Passman, M. Kessler, for the Joint Distribution Committee;
E. Ueberall; D. Schweitzer.

The meeting was called to order at 4:30 p.m.

I. Mr. Hirschmann referred to the telegram received in
Istanbul from Oficiul de Emigrare (apparently the office for
emigration with which Mr. Zissu is associated), stating that
the Turkish Consulate in Bucharest has received instructions
to issue Turkish transit visas valid only for a sea voyage
from Rumania to Istanbul. No instructions have been received
by them which would permit the recipient, at his option, to
travel by sea or rail.

It was the opinion of the meeting that no steps should be
taken with the Turkish authorities at the present time to request
the Turkish Foreign Office to communicate with the Consulate on
the matter. Inquiry at this time might result in a re-opening
of the question with the Foreign Office, which presumably had
agreed to the issuance of transit visas under certain conditions,
as a contribution toward refugee rescue. If no clarification is
received from Bucharest during the course of the coming week,
consideration will be given to the manner in which the Foreign
Office should be approached.

II. Discussion was had with regard to the Turkish vessel
Salahaldin, which has been in Constanza harbor for approximately
six weeks, waiting to transport refugees to Istanbul.

It was reported that several cables had been dispatched to
Bucharest to inquire regarding the present possibilities for the
departure of the boat with refugees. In the opinion of the Jewish
Agency representatives, a recall of the vessel should be postponed
until such time as definite information is received as to whether
or not a transport can be sent off from Constanza by sea.

-2-

III. Mr. Hirschmann reported that he had discussed informally with Ambassador Steinhardt the requisition by the Russians of the Greek vessel Smyrnic, now in Ismail, Rumania, in accordance with the terms of the Rumanian armistice agreement. This vessel previously had been chartered by the rescue organizations to transport refugees from Rumania to Istanbul. Ambassador Steinhardt saw no basis for American intervention upon which exception to the requisition might be requested of the Russians.

After discussion, it was deemed advisable to hold the question in abeyance until the position regarding emigration from Rumania had been clarified, and until the attitude of the Russians toward emigration from territory controlled by them is better known.

IV. Mr. Ueberall reported on information which had been received from Sofia. According to this information, Jewish as well as non-Jewish Bulgarians are now returning to Sofia.

Although the Bulgarian authorities have advised the Jewish people that they have the right without further authorization to re-enter their former apartments, difficulty exists in having the present Bulgarian inhabitants leave the premises. The Government is lending no assistance in this direction. Blocked bank accounts owned by Jews have been released in part. A special governmental agency has been created to deal with transfers of real property. Part of the difficulty arises because of the administrative chaos which now exists in Sofia, as the re-establishment of authority to meet the new situation has just begun. There is a continuing desire on the part of Jews who have been deprived or, or exhausted, their economic resources during the past few years, to emigrate. Two groups, each of five young people, have attempted to enter Turkey without Turkish transit visas, in accordance with the Turkish Foreign Office agreement on the subject. It is reported that they were turned back in Bulgaria.

After discussion, it was decided to await receipt of further details regarding the circumstances under which the two groups attempted to cross the Bulgarian frontier into Turkey and were returned to Bulgaria, before considering what steps, if any, should be taken in this connection.

V. Mr. Hirschmann explained the status of War Refugee Board efforts to proceed to Sofia or Bucharest. Efforts are being made for Mr. Hirschmann or Mr. Katzki to proceed to Bucharest to explore from there what further steps might be taken by the War Refugee Board for rescue of refugees, particularly those in Hungary. The practicability of rescue from Hungary via Rumania may be questionable, as there may be involved the traversing of the Russian battle-line, which appears to be forming in Transylvania. In any event, it will be necessary to await the receipt of official permission before traveling to Rumania. In the meanwhile, the War Refugee Board will continue to function in Istanbul. Of course, it cannot help people who, by preference, wish to change the country of their domicile. The task of the Board is to rescue people in imminent peril of death, for political, racial, or religious beliefs. Perhaps investigation on the spot in Bulgaria or Rumania may disclose that there are further steps which must be taken within the limits of the Board's authority in behalf of refugees now in those two countries.

The policy and principles under which the Board has been operating have not changed. The only change has been one in the area of activities, as the result of military or other considerations. In the meanwhile, the Board has been assisting Mr. Passman as an American citizen to undertake the preliminary steps for proceeding to Sofia or Bucharest, as the Joint Distribution Committee undoubtedly will play a vital role in relief work in Bulgaria and Rumania.

Although there may be no vital questions arising, Mr. Hirschmann was of the opinion that the weekly meetings of this committee should continue, for the interchange of information and to keep in touch with the members. Such meetings may provide the nucleus for continued inter-agency cooperation, when relief and emigration activities expand. The mechanisms and techniques

-4-

of cooperation, as it exists today, should not be given up.

VI. Mr. Passman stated that he had planned to proceed to Bucharest with the War Refugee Board as soon as official permission therefor had been received by him. Because he does not know how soon this will be possible, he is therefore planning to go to Palestine during the coming week, to remain for a week or ten days for conferences there.

VII. It was decided that the next meeting of the committee should take place in one week, on September 29.

There being no further business, the meeting was adjourned at 5:30.

Herbert Katzki

HK/b

MINUTES

of a meeting
of the Operating Group of Relief Organizations
at the office of the War Refugee Board, Istanbul
October 2, 1944.

Those present: I. A. Hirschmann, Herbert Katzki, Ehud Ueberall,
Mordecai Kessler, David Schweitzer, Mnachim Bader, and J. Goldin.

The meeting was called to order at 11 a.m.

1. Mr. Hirschmann informed the committee that he had been
recalled to Washington for consultation by the War Refugee Board,
as the result of the changed situation in the Balkan area. He
had asked the committee to meet in order that he might have the
advantage of any last-minute observations or suggestions they
might care to make which he could carry with him to Washington.
He expressed his thanks to the members of the committee for their
helpful cooperation, advice, and assistance, which they as representatives of their respective organizations and individually had
extended to him during the time he was in Turkey. He assured
them that the work of the War Refugee Board would continue in
Turkey, and advised them that Mr. Katzki, who has been vested
with full powers and who has the backing SUPPORT of the American Embassy
and Consulate General, would continue the War Refugee Board programs in this area.

2. Dr. Goldin reported that Mr. Bader and he had obtained a
letter from Bulgarian Minister Balabanoff in Ankara, officially
confirming the statements of policy which had been broadcast
recently over Radio Sofia, relating to the treatment of Jewish
people in Bulgaria. This letter covered the following points:

(a) The Bulgarian frontier authorities have been advised
of the authorization of the Turkish Government to permit the entry
into Turkey for emigration to Palestine of all Jewish people
presenting themselves at the Bulgarian frontier.

(b) The Bulgarian Government has authorized the Bulgarian
Legation in Bucharest to issue Bulgarian transit visas to any
applicant in Rumania who wishes to travel through Bulgaria en
route to Palestine. This instruction to the Bulgarian Legation

likewise authorizes the issuance of Bulgarian transit visas to Jewish people from Hungary and Poland.

(c) The Bulgarian Government has issued regulations contemplating the return to Jewish people in Bulgaria of properties which had been expropriated, and for payment of compensation for properties lost. In addition, funds will be made available for the re-establishment of Jewish schools and social institutions.

3. Mr. Bader, based upon information which he had received, expressed his opinion that the present Bulgarian Government would not be strong, and that one should not depend solely on the official statements made by Bulgarian authorities as an indication that the problems of Jewish people of that country have been resolved and their difficulties terminated. The problem of reconstruction and rehabilitation will be very long and drawn out. Although promises have been made to the Jewish people, a very large proportion of the latter are without resources. This may continue for some time before the Bulgarian Government itself is in a position to aid them. Furthermore, the future of Jewish people who had lost their positions is obscure, as the promised reinstatement of Jewish people to their former economic status is very complicated. He suggested, therefore, the need for continuing emigration and providing assistance to the Jewish people while still in Bulgaria. He recommended consideration of the advisability of extending a loan to the Bulgarian Government, specifically to assist it in carrying out its representations concerning the rehabilitation of Jewish people.

There has been no recent information from Rumania. The position of Rumanian Jewry may be the same as that of Bulgarian Jewry. In Mr. Bader's opinion, it may be necessary to take special steps for emigration of refugees in that country, for the Transnistrian children, etc.

Mr. Bader reported that Mr. Krausz, Jewish Agency representative in Budapest, advised the International Red Cross delegate there

-3-

that, of the former Jewish population in Hungary of 800,000, only 200,000 persons still remained in Hungary. Inferentially, despite the assurances given by the Hungarian Government, deportations did continue, as the figure of 200,000 is substantially smaller than the estimates which had been made during August. Most of the 200,000 are now in camps or in concentrated areas, subject to the dangers which attach to such a situation.

Krausz recommends that the International Red Cross establish an observation post in Budapest in order to protect the lives of the Jewish people in Hungary. Mr. Bader's friends in Geneva are attempting this, and he suggests that perhaps Mr. Simond, the International Red Cross delegate in Turkey, might be approached. In the meanwhile, the national Red Cross organizations affiliated with the International Red Cross should support the request for a Budapest observation bureau, in which connection the United States, Great Britain, and perhaps also Sweden can be especially helpful.

Mr. Bader, in behalf of the Jewish Agency, expressed his REGRET sorrow that Mr. Hirschmann was leaving, and the hope that his departure will not be final. He expressed his appreciation for Mr. Hirschmann's great interest and support in the rescue work of the Agency from the Balkan area, without which much less would have been accomplished.

4. Mr. Schweitzer seconded Mr. Bader's expressions with reference to the aid Mr. Hirschmann has given in Turkey and promised, in behalf of the committee, full support to Mr. Katzki during Mr. Hirschmann's absence. He thought it important that Mr. Hirschmann interpret to the larger post-war organizations, such as UNRRA, and the Intergovernmental Committee, the problems which will exist in the Balkans and the need for assistance which will arise when military operations cease. In his opinion, the War Refugee Board should not terminate its activities as soon as an area becomes liberated, in strict construction of its terms of

-4-

reference. The War Refugee Board, as a vital organization, should alter its policy so that its influence and effectiveness can be continued in post-war work.

5. Mr. Goldin reported that he had been approached by individuals among the three or four thousand Turkish nationals who have been repatriated to Turkey from France on the subject of their early return to France. Many of them had substantial interests and resources in France, which made them anxious to return to that country as soon as possible.

It was the opinion of the meeting that the question of improving the condition of Jewish people who have already been saved is of minor importance when compared with the need for rescuing persons whose lives are still in danger. The question of the return to France of repatriated Turkish nationals in Turkey should be deferred until more urgent matters have been met.

6. Mr. Ueberall expressed the appreciation of the groups he represented for the cooperation and support which Mr. Hirschmann and the War Refugee Board extended to them. The work of rescue of Jewish people from countries under Nazi pressure, especially Hungary, is not ended. In addition, regular emigration from Bulgaria and Rumania must be supported. Although the expressed policy of the War Refugee Board is the rescue of persons in imminent peril of death, the work of the Jewish Agency does not end there. The Jewish Agency still has the task of emigration to Palestine, and Mr. Ueberall requested that Mr. Hirschmann explain the situation to the War Refugee Board in Washington, so that the Board and the United States Government continue their interest in normal emigration from liberated areas to Palestine.

7. Mr. Hirschmann promised to inform interested agencies and circles in the United States of the views expressed at this meeting. He suggested that a memorandum be prepared by the agency representatives at the meeting, setting forth the suggestions they had made, so that he can have this in writing for reference purposes

-5-

in Washington. He stated that, at this stage, it is important
that Washington be informed as to the views of people in Istanbul who are close to rescue and relief problems, and he promised
to impart this information. Mr. Hirschmann again thanked the
committee for their cooperation, and expressed his continuing
interest in their activities.

There being no further business, the meeting was adjourned
at 12:15.


Herbert Katzki

MINUTES

of a meeting
of the Operating Group of Relief Organizations
at the office of the War Refugee Board, Istanbul
October 9, 1944

Those present: Herbert Katzki, Mordecai Kessler, David Schweitzer, Ehud Ueberall, J. Goldin, and Mnachim Bader.

The meeting was called to order at 11:30 a.m.

1. Mr. Bader reported the receipt of telegrams originating in Bucharest, requesting that steps be taken to modify the Turkish Foreign Office agreement relating to the issuance of Turkish transit visas by the Turkish Consulate in Rumania to Jewish people emigrating to Palestine. The present agreement provides for the issuance of 400 Turkish transit visas every ten days for the voyage by sea from Constanza and Burgas, to be divided between the Turkish Consulates in those cities. The request was that this arrangement be modified to authorize the issuance of transit visas for land travel from Rumania.

There was full discussion regarding this suggestion, during which Mr. Bader suggested a formula that the modification, if requested, provide for the issuance of transit visas for land travel to the extent that the 400 visas authorized every ten days were unused for sea voyage. In this way, he proposed to avoid requesting a radical change in the agreement which, if sought, might precipitate a reconsideration by the Turkish Foreign Office of the entire agreement.

In view of the fact that there is no information available in Istanbul as to the actual situation in Rumania regarding emigration, the possibility of transportation by sea, railroad, etc., the meeting decided that efforts should be made to secure fuller details before making any requests of the Turkish Foreign Office.

2. As a matter of interest, Mr. Bader reported that the Bulgarian Government will begin shortly to issue exit visas for children emigrating to Palestine under the Children's Scheme. The Jewish Agency in Istanbul regards this information with all reserve.

3. Mr. Katzki reported briefly on the steps heretofore taken by the War Refugee Board in relation to emigration of Jewish people from Hungary.

4. In behalf of the War Refugee Board, Mr. Katzki expressed his thanks to Mr. Schweitzer, who is departing from Istanbul to Palestine, for the advice and aid he extended to the War Refugee Board in connection with the program it has been carrying out in Turkey.

The meeting was adjourned at 12:00 noon.

Herbert Katzki

HK/b

94

INTERPRETATION REPORT D.377A

18.4.44

SORTIE: 60 PR 288

Prints 4028-43, 4046-53

Date of photography: 4.4.44.

Contact Scale: 1/15,500

LOCALITY: OSWIECIM (AUSCHWITZ)

SYNTHETIC RUBBER AND SYNTHETIC OIL PLANT

Map - Poland 1/100,000    50° 02' 20" N.
Sheet 48/28    19° 17' 00" E.

1.  GENERAL

(i)   This sortie provides first cover of the new works under construction
      at OSWIECIM. The works is situated 3 Km. E. of the town, immediately
      South of the village of DWORY.

(ii)  The cover confirms reports that the works includes a power station,
      carbide plant, synthetic rubber plant and synthetic oil (Bergius)
      plant.

(iii) The account which follows is a preliminary statement, and will be
      followed by a detailed report. It has not been submitted to M.E.W.
      before issue.

(iv)  The long axis of the plant lies nearly E-W, the area at present under
      development measuring 9,700 ft. by 4,100 ft. The gas plants, power
      station and carbide plant are situated in line from west to east
      along the northern side of the works; the synthetic oil plant occupies
      the area west of the N-S centre line, and the synthetic rubber plant
      the area to the east of this.

2.  SYNTHETIC OIL PLANT

(i)   The synthetic oil plant shows considerable resemblance to the
      installation at BLECHHAMMER SOUTH. Hydrogen is derived from two
      large plants of water gas type and is purified in sulphur removal
      columns of the usual kind. Conversion is carried out in a plant
      differing from those known elsewhere, but the $CO_2$ washing plant
      and compressor house are normal. A second large compressor house is
      being built, as at BLECHHAMMER-SOUTH.

(ii)  Six stalls (three pairs) have been erected for oil production.
      Four measure 51 x 25 ft. and two 40 x 20 ft. in plan; they appear
      to be short stalls as at BLECHHAMMER-SOUTH. The refinery section
      also resembles that at this plant. No oil storage tanks appear
      to have been constructed on this part of the site. Pipe connections
      have been made throughout the synthetic oil plant.

(iii) If the stalls have similar capacities to those at BLECHHAMMER-SOUTH
      the output from the six erected up to the present would be 180,000-
      200,000 tons. There are sites for a number of other stalls but
      their erection has not begun. As noted below, the synthetic oil
      plant is probably in production, but it is not possible to determine
      how many of the six stalls are in use.

(iv)  It may be noted that there is no sign of coal pasting plant or of
      carbonising ovens, an indication that tar oil residues constitute
      the feedstock.

/3.

## 3. SYNTHETIC RUBBER PLANT.

(i) The general appearance of the buildings at this plant more closely resembles SCHKOPAU than either HÜLS or LUDWIGSHAFEN. Most of the buildings occupied by the various stages of the buna process can be identified by comparison with corresponding buildings at SCHKOPAU and there can be little doubt that the process used is the same.

(ii) The carbide furnace building measures about 325' x 100' which suggests that it contains three furnaces as compared with eight at SCHKOPAU and two at LUDWIGSHAFEN.

(iii) The butylene glycol stalls are in two sets as at the other plants but these are dissimilar in size measuring 96' x 20' and 61' x 20'. It therefore seems probable that one set contains three stalls as at the other plants and the other only two and that the ultimate capacity will be about five-sixths of that of SCHKOPAU or HÜLS. The compressor house for these stalls at present measures about 160' x 60' but it is probably intended to extend it. For the source of hydrogen see 2(i) above.

(iv) What is believed to be a styrene plant can be identified and it is probable also that an acrylonitrile plant is being constructed.

(v) The buildings for some of the stages of the process appear to be complete but it is clear that others, for example the aldol plant, are not and the same appears to be true of the pipe connections. It seems quite possible however, that the plant is already in partial production.

## 4. ACTIVITY

(i) Although it is clear that much construction is still in progress, and may pipe bridges, for example, are still only partially built, a number of sections of the plant are active.

(ii) At the power station one of the three chimneys is smoking (two more have still to be built) and there is a dump of coal or coke near the fuel intake.

(iii) Both the gas plants are completed and have fuel (coke?) in the bunkers. Steam emission is seen at two points in the western plant. Three gashold. have been completed and are nearly full in the synthetic oil section, and steam emission can be seen from a blower house transmitting raw gas to the sulphur plant.

(iv) The large cooling tower serving the main compressor house is steaming, sh... that the compressors are in use and that compressed gas is being passed through the plant. This indicates that oil is being produced and although the absence of storage tanks is an unusual feature (these may have been sit elsewhere for some reason) seven tank wagons are seen on the siding alongside the refinery, and two more ar parked near the western boundary of the works.

(v) The single tall chimney of the carbide plant is smoking freely, but there is no other evidence of manufacturing activity in the buna section of the works.

DISTRIBUTION NO.42

3 : 30    I : 16    Total: 47 copies.
          + 1 D. of Ops. (3.0.)

DECLASSIFIED

INTERPRETATION REPORT NO. D.326R

Sortie 60 PR.522 prints 4043 - 48

Date of Photography: 26th June 1944

Scale: (F.L.36")

OSMIECIM

Activity of I.G.F. Works

## 1. General

Cover of 26.6.44 shows the whole plant on good scale prints.
Although the gas plants are active there is no evidence of production
of synthetic oil.

## 2. Details of Activity of Synthetic Oil Section

(i) Smoke is issuing from one chimney of the boiler house, but
no steam can be detected in the finished cooling tower which
serves the generator hall.

(ii) One generator of the water gas plant has a smoking chimney,
and five gasholders are full. The I.T.C. plant has one
unit in use, and like the gas plant has a heap of fuel near
the coal intake.

(iii) No evidence of use of the remainder of the plant can be
found; in particular the cooling towers serving the
compressor houses are not in use, and there is no traffic
activity.

(iv) Three of the six stalls may be partly equipped, although it
is not possible to be certain how far this is complete.
Construction of the additional six stalls is in progress.

## 3. Activity of Synthetic Rubber Section

(i) Since 4.4.44 (60 PR 288) considerable progress has been
made with the rubber section. A second kiln has been
completed and the third is well advanced. The aldol
plant has advanced

/plant has advanced

28.7.44.

- 2 -

plant has advanced considerably and a distillation column has been installed there. Progress in construction elsewhere has also been considerable.

(ii) The chimney of the carbide plant is smoking though much less vigorously than on previous sorties. The probable acetylene gasholder is full. Railway wagons are seen near the acetaldehyde plant but not near the buildings connected with the later stages of production. For the activity of the boiler house and gas plant see para. 2 above.

(iii) It seems probable that the synthetic rubber section is now working at about half its planned capacity (i.e. at a rate of about 10,000 tons a year).

SECRET
A.C.I.U.
PEK/EFW/MF/B

DISTRIBUTION NO.19
E:  21
I:  18
    29

MEDITERRANEAN ALLIED PHOTO
RECONNAISSANCE WING

30 August 1944

INTERPRETATION REPORT No. DP.95

Photographs taken by 60 Squadron on 23rd & 25th August 1944.

SORTIES:  60 PR 686.
          6C PR 694.

SCALES :  1/9,700 Approx. (F.L. 36")
          1/10,000 Approx. (F.L. 36")

CJ-5212

POLAND

LOCALITY: OSWIECIM (AUSCHWITZ)

I. G.F. Synthetic Rubber & Synthetic Oil Plant.

COVER; Prints are of good scale & quality.

ATTACKED: 20 August 1944 by 15th Air Force.

REPORTS: DE 189, of 23 August 1944.
         DE 191, or 25 August 1944.

1. DAMAGE. (This report deals with the synthetic oil refinery, but the plan issued is of the whole works. It will be seen that the greater part of the damage was done in the synthetic rubber plant. Interpretation has been done mainly on sortie 60 PR 686. On sortie 60 PR 694, of 2 days later, some slight clearance & repairs are seen.)

PRIMARY OBJECTIVES. (Numbers in parenthesis refer to plan distributed).

a. Boiler house & generator hall, with switch & transformer house: No damage seen. (10 and 11)

b. Water gas plant, with blower house: no damage seen. (8 and 58)

c. H2S removal plant: no damage seen. (73)

d. CO2 & CO removal plant: small installation partly wrecked. (80)

e. Gas conversion plant:  no damage seen. (81)

f. Injector houses:  no damage seen. (83 and 84)

2. SECONDARY OBJECTIVES

a. Distillation units:  1 small building destroyed. (98)

b. Compressor houses:  the E. end of a compressor house is slightly damaged. (75)

3. OTHER INSTALLATIONS

a. Probable methanol plant:  the building is about ⅓ badly damaged. (61)

b. The purified gasholder and another gasholder have been damaged by blast. (64 and 70)

c. Several workshops, storehouses, living huts, and some buildings which are still under construction, have suffered varying degrees of damage.

d. Several instances of further construction since 26 June are seen.

Cont'd page 2.

## ACTIVITY

There are no signs of operational activity on the photographs of 23 August, but on 25 August signs of activity include steam issuing from 4 or vents of the water gas plant. Smoke can be seen in various parts of the pl but since several smoke generators are in action around the perimeter of t plant, it is believed that the source of smoke at most of the internal poi is also the smoke generation system. There is the usual amount of M.T. and personnel activity. Rail activity however, is largely limited to to movement of cars other than tank cars, only 7 to 10 of the latter being so

## SUMMARY

Apparently this plant has not as yet come into production. The damage received is not sufficient to interfere seriously with synthetic fuel production, and should not greatly delay completion of this part of the pl

Prints: 60PR/686:- 3067 to 3075
60PR/694:- 4172 to 4178

Comparative: 60PR/522:- 4044 to 4048.

Prints distributed:- 60PR/694, 4173,41    41

Plan distributed:- Copy of A.I.C.U. pl
No. D.410, altered
show damage.

DISTRIBUTION 'D.P.'
External..........13
Internal...........7

IG/FFB/BQ

100

S E C R E T

# E X T R A C T

WAR CABINET TECHNICAL SUB-COMMITTEE ON AXIS OIL REPORTS, dated 27th May 1944

## BERGIUS HYDROGENATION PLANTS

Oswiecim-63612 7

AUSCHWITZ:

The hydrogenation section at the new plant at Auschwitz is only just coming into use. When the construction now in progress has been completed the output of this plant may be at the rate of 180,000 tons per annum. The planned capacity of the plant is probably to the order of half a million tons per annum.

## OIL REFERENCE DATA

The oil position in Axis Europe first 6 months of 1944: Refer to War Cabinet Technical Sub-Committe on Axis Oil, AO (44) 41. Final, dtd 27 May 1944

Published by - Offices of the War Cabinet S.W. 1, 27 May 1944.

SECRET

NOV 15 1944

Combined Routing - Information - Filing Form

Operations Division

War Department Decimal Classification: OPD CCS.5 (8 Nov 44)

383.6 (Germany)

11-11/1160

SUSPENSE DATE: 13 Nov 44

Origin    War Refugee Bd

X 334.8 War Refugee Bd
X 095 McCloy, John J.
X 091 Germany
X 020.1

Subject: Eye-witness Descriptions of the German Concentration and Extermination Camps  8 Nov 44
of Auschwitz and Birkenau.

Digest: ltr from War Refugee Bd to Mr. McCloy, 8 Nov 44, forwards subject reports and
requests views of the OD regarding the suggestion that these camps be bombed. (Memo
slip from Office Asst Secy/War, 9 Nov 44, forwards for remark and recommendation)

Action:

Memorandum to Ass't Secretary of War prepared for General Hull's
signature containing remarks and recommendations on the letter from Executive
Director, War Refugee Board to Mr. McCloy.

| | | Strategy Section |
| --- | --- | --- |
| Comments: | | |
| Recommendation: | | |
| | Section Chief | Date 13 Nov 44 |
| | Group Chief | Date |
| Concurrence: | | |

☐ Asiatic
☐ European
☐ Latin American
☐ Liaison
☐ Middle East - Cen. Africa    ☐ Theaters
☐ North African
☐ North American
☐ Pacific
☐ Southwest Pacific
☐ Troop Movements
☐ Troop
☐ Materiel    ☐ Logistics
☐ Plans & Asmt.
☐ Policy    ☐ Strategy &
☐ Strategy          Policy
☐ Current    ☐ A. C. of Staff
☐ Reg. Doc.    ☐ Deputy A. C. of Staff
☐ Executive, OPD
☐ Dispatch Desk { ☐ Dispatch
                  ☐ File

Action by Col. Crosthwaite

Date 13 Nov 44

Signed

Doc. 5

102

EXECUTIVE OFFICE OF THE PRESIDENT
War Refugee Board
Washington 25, D.C.

Nov 8 1944

Dear Mr. McCloy:

I send you herewith copies of two eye-witness descriptions of the notorious German concentration and extermination camps of Auschwitz and Birkenau in Upper Silesia, which have just been received from the Board's Special Representative in Bern, Switzerland, Roswell McClelland whom we have borrowed from the American Friends Service Committee. No report of Nazi atrocities received by the Board has quite caught the gruesome brutality of what is taking place in these camps of horror as have these sober, factual accounts of conditions in Auschwitz and Birkenau. I earnestly hope that you will read these reports.

The destruction of large numbers of people apparently is not a simple process. The Germans have been forced to devote considerable technological ingenuity and administrative know-how in order to carry out murder on a mass production basis, as the attached reports will testify. If the elaborate murder installations at Birkenau were destroyed, it seems clear that the Germans could not reconstruct them for some time.

Until now, despite pressure from many sources, I have been hesitant to urge the destruction of these camps by direct, military action. But I am convinced that the point has now been reached where such action is justifiable if it is deemed feasible by competent military authorities. I strongly recommend that the War Department give serious consideration to the possibility of destroying the execution chambers and crematories in Birkenau through direct bombing action. It may be observed that there would be other advantages of a military nature to such an attack. The Krupp and Siemens factories, where among other things cases for handgrenades are made, and a Buna plant, all within Auschwitz, would be destroyed. The destruction of the German barracks and guard-houses and the killing of German soldiers in the area would also be accomplished. The morale of underground groups might be considerably strengthened by such a dramatic exhibition of Allied air support and a number of the people confined in Auschwitz and Birkenau might be liberated in the confusion resulting from the bombing. That the effecting of a prison break by such methods is not without precedent is indicated by the description in the enclosed copy of a recent New York Times article of the liberation from Amiens prison of 100 French patriots by the RAF.

STRATEGY & POLICY FILE COPY

Obviously, the War Refugee Board is in no position to determine whether the foregoing proposal is feasible from a military standpoint. Nevertheless in view of the urgency of the situation, we feel justified in making the suggestion. I would appreciate having the views of the War Department as soon as possible.

Very truly yours,

/s/ J. W. Pehle

J. W. Pehle
Executive Director

Honorable John J. McCloy,

Assistant Secretary of War.

Enclosures.

104

THE NEW YORK TIMES -- Sunday, October 29, 1944
(Section I, Page 7, Columns 1-3)

PRISON BREAK DONE BY RAF AT AMIENS

Bomb Freeing of Doomed French, in Which Capt. P. C. Pickard Was
Killed, Revealed

by

Sydney Gruson

"London, Oct. 28 -- Last Feb. 18 a picked group of nineteen pinpoint
Mosquito bombers of the Royal Air Force, led by Group Capt. P. C. Pickard,
broke down the walls of Amiens Prison, shattered the Germans' guard houses
and enabled most of one hundred French patriots awaiting probable death to
escape.

"The British Air Ministry released tonight the story of this unique
exploit, one of the most difficult ever accomplished by the RAF, and announced that it was during this operation that Captain Pickard, the famous
F for Freddie pilot of the film 'Target for Tonight' and ranked as the
RAF's finest bomber pilot, was killed.

"At the briefing just before they took off Captain Pickard told his
men: 'It's a death-or-glory job, boys.' It meant death for Captain Pickard
and his observer and the crews of a second Mosquito and two fighter escorts
that failed to return.

"Three squadrons of Mosquito bombers escorted by Spitfires were sent
to do the job -- the only time an air force has been used to unlock a jail.
The prison was a cruciform building in a courtyard surrounded by a wall
twenty feet high and three feet thick. The walls had to be breached and
the German quarters destroyed, the latter with as little explosive as possible
to keep casualties to a minimum among the French men in the adjoining prison.

"A model of the prison was carefully studied by all the airmen. Taking
off from a snow-covered airfield, the three squadrons got to Amiens dead on
time and found a break in the clouds over the area.

"A New Zealand squadron went in first and breached the wall on its
northeast and northwest perimeter. The second wave of six bombers, flown
by Australians, divided and slit open the jail by smashing the guard's
annexes at both ends. The third squadron held in reserve, never had to be
used, so exactly and thoroughly did the New Zealanders and Australians do
the job.

- 1 -

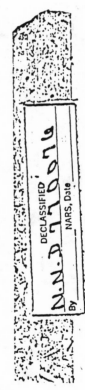

and out. A photographic plane made three runs over the prison and brought back film showing the prisoners running out through the breaches in the build-ing and walls, Germans lying dead on the ground and patriots disappearing across the snow on a field outside the prison.

"Although some of the Frenchmen were killed by the machine-guns of the Nazi guards, the Air Ministry learned that the majority of them got away, joining up with members of the underground awaiting them in a near-by woods.

"After Amiens was liberated, the French told how Captain Pickard died. He had detached his plane from the main force and protecting fighters to direct and observe the assault. When one Mosquito was hit by German flak, he flew low, apparently to investigate the fate of the crew.

"Two Focke-Wulf 190's attacked his plane and shot it down a few miles from Amiens. He and his crewmen were buried by the Germans in a cemetery alongside the prison.

"'The feeling of the men in our squadron, and it was the same with the others, was that this was a job where it did not matter if we were all killed,' said one of the Australian pilots.

"It was the sort of operation that gave you a feeling that, if you did nothing else in this war, you had done something.'"

"The Mosquitos used delayed-action bombs and skimmed the walls going in

OPD 000.5 (8 Nov 44)

14 November 1944

MEMORANDUM FOR THE ASSISTANT SECRETARY OF WAR:

Subject: Suggestion by the Executive Director, War
Refugee Board, for the Aerial Bombing of
German Concentration Camps Located at
Auschwitz and Birkenau in Upper Silesia.

1. The Executive Director of the War Refugee Board suggests the bombing of these German concentration and extermination camps largely from a humanitarian standpoint but includes incidental military advantages to be gained through the destruction of war industrial factories within the area of the target. In considering this proposal, the following points were considered:

a. Positive destruction of these camps would necessitate precision bombing, employing heavy or medium bombardment, or attack by low flying or dive bombing aircraft, preferably the latter.

b. The target is beyond the maximum range of medium bombardment, dive bombers and fighter bombers located in United Kingdom, France or Italy.

c. Use of heavy bombardment from United Kingdom bases would necessitate a round trip flight unescorted of approximately 2000 miles over enemy territory.

d. At the present critical stage of the war in Europe, our strategic air forces are engaged in the destruction of industrial target systems so vital to our effort that we cannot afford diversion. The targets suggested are not a part of these target systems and therefore the military value of the proposed effort is doubtful. The positive solution to this problem is the earliest possible victory over Germany, to which end we should exert our entire means.

e. This case does not appear to parallel that stated by the Executive Director of the War Refugee Board because of the location of the concentration and extermination camps and the resulting difficulties encountered in attempting to carry out the proposed bombing.

-1-

2. Based on the above, it is necessary to conclude that the proposal is of very doubtful feasibility and is unacceptable from a military standpoint at this time in that it would be a diversion from our strategic bombing effort and the results obtained would not justify the high losses likely to result from such a mission.

3. It is recommended that the Executive Director of the War Refugee Board be informed substantially, as above.

J. E. HULL,
Major General,
Assistant Chief of Staff.

rg

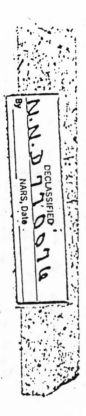

ABC 383.6 (8 Nov 43) Sec. 1A

14 November 1944

Suggestion by Emergency Director War Refugee Bd for the aerial bombing of German concentration camps loated at AUCHWITZ and BIRKENAU in Upper Silesia.

Note General Hull's memo to Ass't S/W, par. 2 "---it is necessary to conclude that the proposal is of very doubtful feasibility and is unacceptable from a military standpoint at this time in that it would be a diversion from our strategic bombing effort and the results obtained would not justify the high losses likely to result from such a mission."

The two ey-witness descriptions of the concentration camps referred to in the War Refugee Bd letter to McCloy (Nov 8, 44) were not attached to the file. The reference to a New York Times article concerning a Prison Break by RAF at Amiens was attached.

TO:    Assistant Secretary McCloy

FROM:  Secretary Morgenthau

In accordance with your timely suggestion it would be very helpful if instructions along the following lines were sent to the appropriate Theater Commanders:

"The President has instructed the Secretaries of State, Treasury and War to take action for the immediate rescue and relief of the Jews of Europe and other victims of enemy persecution. In an Executive Order issued January 22, 1944, the President declared 'it is the policy of this Government to take all measures within its power to rescue the victims of enemy oppression who are in imminent danger of death and otherwise to afford such victims all possible relief and assistance consistent with the successful prosecution of the war.' The order establishes special governmental machinery for executing this policy. It creates a War Refugee Board consisting of the Secretaries of State, Treasury and War. The Board is charged with direct responsibility to the President in seeing that the announced policy is carried out. The President indicated that while he would look directly to the Board for the execution of this policy, the Board would cooperate with the Inter-governmental Committee, UNRRA, and other interested international organiza- tions. The President stated that he expected the cooperation of all members of the United Nations and other governments in carrying out this difficult but important task. He stated that the existing facilities of the State, Treasury and War Departments would be employed to furnish aid to Axis victims to the fullest extent possible. He stressed that it was urgent that action be taken to forestall the plot of the Nazis to exterminate the Jews and other persecuted minorities in Europe.

You should do everything possible, consistent with the successful prosecution of the war in your theater, to effectuate this policy of this Government. You should cooperate as closely as possible with all public and established private agencies who are active in your theater in this field in this matter. Consistent with your needs and military security considerations, you should make communication facilities avail- able to these private agencies for appropriate messages for carrying out the policy of this Government herein stated, keeping the War Refugee Board advised through the Department. You should report to the Department any recommendations which you may have as to what you feel this Department can do to effectuate with all possible speed the rescue and relief of the victims of enemy oppression.

Doc. 6

110

#4

Foreign representatives of the Department of State and of other Government Departments are being similarly instructed and you should give them any possible assistance."

I would appreciate your bringing this to the attention of Secretary Stimson.

/s/ Henry Morgenthau, Jr.

Jan.28, 1944.

112

## PARAPHRASE OF CABLE

SINCE APRIL, WE ARE RECEIVING DESPAIRED LETTERS AND CABLES ABOUT THE DEPORTATION OF THE JEWS FROM HUNGARY AND SLOVAKIA TO POLAND, WHICH NATURALLY MEANS TO DEATH. OFTEN, FROM 10 TO 15 THOUSAND PEOPLE ARE DEPORTED DAILY. ALTOGETHER, ABOUT 300,000 PERSONS HAVE BEEN DEPORTED SO FAR. WE HAVE ASKED, IN THE AMERICAN AND BRITISH LEGATIONS FOR THE BOMBARDMENT OF THE GIVEN RAIL-HUB POINTS (KASHAU-PRESSOV) BUT SO FAR WITHOUT RESULTS. THE WHOLE RELIEF ACTION, COMMISARS, PITY, ETC., ARE USELESS UNLESS DECISIVE STEPS ARE BEING UNDERTAKEN.

PLEASE INTERVENE IMMEDIATELY WITH PRESIDENT ROOSEVELT, CHURCHILL AND EVENTUALLY IN MOSCOW, TO BOMBARD THE GIVEN POINTS AS SOON AS POSSIBLE, WHICH ALONE COULD SAVE THESE PEOPLE.

THE RESPONSIBILITY FOR THE CAUSING OF THIS EXPERIMENT IS TREMENDOUS. PLEASE CONSIDER ALL THIS VERY DISCREETLY.

Proposed Air Action to Impede Deportation of    23 June 1944.
Hungarian and Slovak Jews


X  OPD


X. Necessary action


1. The inclosed paraphrase of a cable concerning the proposed air bombardment of the railroad centers of Kashau-Pressov to impede the deportation of Jews from Hungary and Slovakia to Poland was forwarded to this Division for consideration and appropriate action by Mr. Morgenthau, the Chairman of the War Refugee Board, at the suggestion of the Executive Director of the Board, Mr. John Pehle.

2. It is requested that the Civil Affairs Division be informed of the action taken.


J. H. HILLDRING,
Major General,
Director, Civil Affairs Division.


CHAS. L KADES
Lt Colonel, GSC
Asst Executive


Incl.
Paraphrase of cable

113

OPD 383.7 (23 Jun 44)

MEMO FOR RECORD:

Subject: Proposed Air Action to Impede Deportation of
Hungarian and Slovak Jews.

In a letter to the Assistant Secretary of War from the Secretary
of the Treasury, dated 28 January 1944, Secretary Morgenthau makes
reference to the creation, by Executive Order, of a War Refugee Board
consisting of the Secretaries of State, Treasury and War. This Board
is charged with direct responsibility to the President in carrying out the
policy of this Government to take all measures within its power to rescue
victims of enemy oppression. This letter was referred to the Deputy
Chief of Staff, and in reply the Deputy Chief of Staff in a memo for the
Assistant Secretary of War stated: "We must constantly bear in mind however
that the most effective relief which can be given victims of enemy
persecution is to insure the speedy defeat of the Axis. For this reason,
I share your concern over further involvement of the War Department,
while the war is on, in matters such as the one brought up by Secretary
Morgenthau." (See OPD 334.8 War Refugee Board, 28 Jan 44).

By memorandum dated 7 February 44 Lt. Col. Pasco, Assistant Secretary
General Staff, informed Colonel Galley that the British have informed
Mr. Morgenthau that they are reluctant to cooperate with the War Refugee
Board because the membership of the Secretary of War implies that units
or individuals of the armed forces will be used in rescuing refugees.
Mr. Bundy, who represents the S/W on this Board, requested OPD concurrence
to transmission of the following message to the British Government:

"It is not contemplated that such military missions as
parachute troop movements will be employed to rescue victims
of enemy oppression."

This matter was submitted to General Hull for decision and General Hull
agreed to the following message:

"It is not contemplated that units of the armed forces will
be employed for the purpose of rescuing victims of enemy oppression
unless such rescues are the direct result of military operations
conducted with the objective of defeating the armed forces of the
enemy." (See OPD 334.8 War Refugee Board, 7 Feb 44).

CAD/D/F dated 23 June 44 forwards to OPD for necessary action paraphrase of cable concerning air bombardment of railroad centers to impede
deportation of Jews to Poland, which message had been forwarded to the CAD
by Mr. McCloy. As this message was referred to the Civil Affairs Division
by Mr. McCloy for appropriate action, the Operations Division does not
consider that it is appropriate for OPD to make reply. Therefore, action
taken by OPD was to furnish CAD with a suggested reply to be made by CAD.

T.R.H.        COPY FOR OPD FILE

114

CONFIDENTIAL
TRH. 71932.G.S.

Ext. 71932.G.S.

OPD 383.7 (23 Jun 44)

26 June 1944

Proposed Air Action to Impede Deportation of Hungarian
and Slovak Jews.

X Director, CAD

X Necessary Action

1. Reference is made to Civil Affairs Division disposition form, subject as above, dated 23 June 1944, which forwarded to the Operations Division for necessary action a paraphrase of a cable on the above subject.

2. The Operations Division, WDGS, recommends that the Civil Affairs Division reply to Mr. Morgenthau, the Chairman of the War Refugee Board, substantially as follows:

"The War Department is of the opinion that the suggested air operation is impracticable for the reason that it could be executed only by diversion of considerable air support essential to the success of our forces now engaged in decisive operations.

"The War Department fully appreciates the humanitarian importance of the suggested operation. However, after due consideration of the problem, it is considered that the most effective relief to victims of enemy persecution is the early defeat of the Axis, an undertaking to which we must devote every resource at our disposal."

3. A copy of this D/F, with identical inclosure, has been furnished CG, AAF and AC/S, G-2.

JUN 28 P.M.

J. E. HULL,
Major General,
Chief, Theater Grs. ...... .,
for THOS. T. HANDY,
Major General,
Assistant Chief of Staff.

1 Incl:
Paraphrase of cable

OUT CONFIDENTIAL
WDGSCENTIAL

OPD                    COPY FOR OPD FILE

mec

EXECUTIVE OFFICE OF THE PRESIDENT

WAR REFUGEE BOARD
WASHINGTON 25, D. C.

JUN 29 1944

TO:   Mr. McCloy, Assistant Secretary of War

FROM:  J. W. Pehle

In connection with my recent conversation with you, I am attaching a copy of a cable just received from our representative in Bern, Switzerland. I wish to direct your attention particularly to the paragraphs concerning the railway lines being used for the deportation of Jews from Hungary to Poland and the proposal of various agencies that vital sections of these lines be bombed.

Attachment:

Operations Division

War Department Decimal Classification: OPD 333.7 (23 Jun 44)

X 000.31
X 353.4
X 017
X 031

X 321.19 CAD
X 091 Hungary
X 091 Poland
X 091 Czechoslovakia
X 291.2

THIS COPY OF ROUTING FORM TO BE RETURNED ONLY BY OPD RECORD SECTION

Date 23 Jun 44   Origin   CAD
SUSPENSE DATE: 30 Jun 44

Subject: Proposed Air Action to Impede Deportation of Hungarian and Slovak Jews.

Digest: CAD D/F, 23 Jun 44, forwards for necessary action, paraphrases of a cable re proposed air bombardment of the railroad centers of Kashau-Presov to impede the deportation of Jews from Hungary and Slovakia to Poland.

Action: OPD D/F to Director, CAD, recommending that CAD prepare reply to Secretary of Treasury indicating War Department disapproval of proposed operation. Copy of D/F with paraphrase of cable furnished CG, AAF and AC/S, G-2, and NATO Theater Section, OPD, for information. No other action necessary.

Policy        Section

Comments:   DECLASSIFIED
E.O. 11652, Sec. 3(E) and 5(D) or (E)
OSD letter, May 3, 1972
By F.A. ___ NARS, Date 12-27-73

Recommendation:                    25 JUN 1944

Section Chief _____ Date _____
Group Chief _____ Date _____

Concurrence:

☐ Executive, OPD
☐ Deputy A.C. of Staff
☐ A.C. of Staff

28 JUN 1944
Theaters
@ TEH on D/F

☐ American
☐ Asiatic
☑ European
☐ Liaison
☐ Middle East-Cen.Africa
☐ North African
☐ Pacific
☐ Southwest Pacific
☐ Troop Movements
☐ Executive
☐ Operational
☐ Projected
☐ Strategy
☐ Current Group
☐ Reg. Doc.

☐ Logistics
☐ Strategy & Policy

☑ Dispatch Desk   Dispatch { ☑ Dispatch  ☐ File }

Action by Lt. Col. Hannah
Signed _____ Date 26 June 1944

24-68681ABC Roo

4 July 1944

Mr. John W. Pehle
Executive Director
War Refugee Board
Treasury Department
Washington 25, D. C.

Dear Mr. Pehle:

I refer to your letter of June 29, inclosing a cable from your representative in Bern, Switzerland, proposing that certain sections of railway lines between Hungary and Poland be bombed to interrupt the transportation of Jews from Hungary.

The War Department is of the opinion that the suggested air operation is impracticable. It could be executed only by the diversion of considerable air support essential to the success of our forces now engaged in decisive operations and would in any case be of such very doubtful efficacy that it would not amount to a practical project.

The War Department fully appreciates the humanitarian motives which prompted the suggested operation but for the reasons stated above the operation suggested does not appear justified.

Sincerely,

(SIGNED) JOHN J. McCLOY

John J. McCloy

3 July 1944

MEMORANDUM FOR MR. McCLOY:

I know you told me to "kill" this
but since those instructions, we have
received the attached letter from Mr. Pehle.

I suggest that the attached reply be sent.

H.A.G.

EXECUTIVE OFFICE OF THE PRESIDENT

WAR REFUGEE BOARD

WASHINGTON 25, D. C.

JUL 15 1944

OFFICE OF THE
EXECUTIVE DIRECTOR

MEMORANDUM FOR THE MEMBERS
OF THE WAR REFUGEE BOARD

COPY FOR
SECRETARY STIMSON

In view of the understandably widespread concern with the plight of the Jews in Hungary, I feel it appropriate to inform you of the known facts of the situation and the steps we have taken in our efforts to meet it.

Ever since the occupation of Hungary by the Germans and the establishment of a puppet government there we have been urgently concerned with the situation of the Jews in that country. Some indication of the unspeakably tragic plight of these people is furnished by the Board's representatives in Sweden and Switzerland in recent cables, copies of several of which are attached.

From many sources we have received heartbreaking pleas and proposals for action. Each of these proposals has been carefully weighed and, where practicable, immediately acted upon. The attached memorandum summarizes our more significant activities with respect to this problem.

In spite of all our concern and our activities there has been no noticeable lessening in the program of persecution and extermination of Jews in Hungary.

We shall, of course, continue to push forward in all our efforts.

J. W. Pehle
Executive Director

Attachments

SUMMARY OF STEPS TAKEN BY WAR REFUGEE BOARD
WITH RESPECT TO THE JEWS OF HUNGARY

Immediately upon the German occupation of Hungary with its indication of increased brutality to Jews and other minorities in that country, the programs of the War Refugee Board were geared to the urgency of the situation and our efforts have been unstinting to forestall deportations and executions and to rescue as many as possible of these victims. Every suggestion, from private as well as public sources, has been carefully analyzed and studied by the Board and every possible project to save these people has been vigorously pursued. The full power of the Board has been utilized with respect to the Hungarian situation in the effort to carry out this Government's determined policy to save these Nazi-oppressed peoples.

Our first step was an attempt to get the facts of the situation and urgent cables were immediately despatched to our missions in the neutral countries as well as to the Vatican requesting detailed information on the treatment of Jews in Hungary.

Efforts to Increase Protection to Jews of Hungary

With the receipt of reports that the Germans with the eager assistance of the puppet Hungarian Government were pursuing a program similar to those already undertaken in Poland and elsewhere, we commenced a series of measures designed to obtain some measure of protection for these people in Hungary. We instructed our representatives in the neutral countries to request the Governments to which they are accredited to increase to the largest possible extent the number of their diplomatic and consular personnel in Hungary in the hope that such representatives would use all means available to persuade individuals and officials in Hungary to desist in the persecution of Jews. Turkey, Portugal, Spain and Switzerland did not respond favorably to this appeal. Sweden, in view of the humanitarian considerations, agreed wholeheartedly and immediately arranged for extra diplomatic personnel in Hungary.

- 2 -

The International Red Cross was also urged to increase its representation in Hungary in order to protect the well-being of the groups in that country facing persecution. While the reaction to this request was unfavorable at first, upon our repeated urging the International Red Cross now appears to be attempting to arrange for additional personnel in Hungary and they are cooperating with our representative in Switzerland in his efforts to help the Jews of Hungary.

At the urgent request of the Board, a cable was sent to the Vatican in the name of the Government of the United States calling the attention of the Holy See to the reports of persecution in Hungary and calling upon the Pope to express himself on the subject to the authorities and people of Hungary personally by radio and through the clergy in Hungary. The cable also urged that His Holiness might find it possible to remind the people of Hungary of the spiritual consequences of the acts being perpetrated in Hungary and that the Vatican send extra representation into Hungary. The Apostolic Delegate has just advised us that on June 25th the Pope addressed a personal appeal to Regent Horthy to do everything possible in favor of these unfortunate persons suffering because of their race or nationality. Horthy responded that he would do everything in his power to cause the demands of humanitarian and Christian principles to prevail. In addition, the Apostolic Delegate advises that the Apostolic Nunciature in Budapest has been carrying on intense activity in behalf of the non-Aryan Hungarians and in every way is seeking to aid and protect them.

At the urgent request of the Board, Minister Harrison was asked to request the Swiss Government to address an inquiry in the name of the United States Government to the appropriate Hungarian authorities asking them to state their intentions with respect to the future treatment to be accorded Jews and to remind such authorities of the grave view this Government takes concerning the persecution of Jews and other minorities. The note containing this message was delivered to the Hungarian Foreign Office by the Swiss on June 27th.

Intensification of Psychological Warfare Program

In cooperation with OWI, arrangements have been made to beam messages continually to Hungary warning her people and officials to desist in persecuting the Jews and informing them of our determination to punish the perpetrators of such cruelties. OWI coverage has been very widespread from overseas as well as from the United States. The British and Russian Governments were immediately urged to cooperate in this psychological program by increased broadcasts to the Satellites.

The President's statement of March 24th on Nazi atrocities was repeatedly used in broadcasts from this country. Through our efforts the members of the Senate Foreign Relations Committee signed a strong statement condemning the brutal treatment of Jews in Hungary and the House Foreign Affairs Committee followed suit by unanimously approving a resolution condemning the German persecution of minorities and, in particular, the barbarous acts being pursued in Hungary. These two statements have been used over and over again in OWI programs to occupied Europe. Through War Refugee Board representatives abroad the texts of these statements were made available to the press and radio of neutral countries. A statement decrying the Nazi atrocities signed by Governor Alfred E. Smith and 70 other prominent American Christians has been given similar coverage throughout the world.

Recently, at our request, Archbishop Spellman of New York, in an unprecedented move, issued a stirring spiritual appeal to the people of Hungary to desist in submitting to the lust and tyranny of the Nazi extermination program. This statement has been hailed by people all over the world and has been radioed repeatedly to Hungary and the other satellite countries from the United States and the neutral countries. Pamphlets containing the Archbishop's statement and the other statements mentioned above have been dropped by planes over Hungary in an attempt to reach as many people as possible.

124

## Operations from Sweden

The Swedish Foreign Office has cooperated closely with our representative and has made available to him various official reports received from Swedish diplomatic personnel in Hungary. In addition, the Swedish Foreign Office has arranged to send Mr. Wallenberg, a prominent Swedish business man, to Budapest as attache in refugee matters with the express purpose of saving as many lives as possible. The Swedish Foreign Office has gone so far as to indicate that Wallenberg would be available for any work the War Refugee Board might wish to assign to him. We have, of course, cabled that, while Wallenberg could not act as the Board's representative nor in its name, he is free to communicate with our representative in Stockholm and to lay before him any specific proposals to aid the Jews of Hungary. Our representative has been instructed to lend every assistance possible to this mission.

In the hope that rescue operations might be increased and developed from Sweden, we have sent a detailed program to Olsen suggesting the names of persons in Hungary who might be helpful in arranging rescues and we have indicated various escape routes which might be available from Hungary. We have arranged for private funds to be sent to Olsen to be used expressly for rescue operations from Hungary and we have indicated our willingness and eagerness to discuss any suggestion or program designed to help the persecuted people of Hungary.

## Operations from Switzerland

Board representative, McClelland, has received instructions similar to those sent to Olsen and he has been requested to coordinate the activities of American organizations in Switzerland in an effort to ensure the most effective rescue operations for Hungarian Jews. Names of individuals in Hungary who may be of assistance and possible escape routes have been sent to him. In response to McClelland's urgent request for funds to finance the rescue of Nazi victims from Hungary, the Board arranged for remittances of $1,125,000 of private funds, to Switzerland. Through a special appeal to the Swiss Minister, arrangements were made for the Swiss authorities to make the necessary Swiss francs available for these activities. McClelland has reported to the Board that numerous operations are now under way and that all reports and appeals from the Jews of Hungary are given careful consideration in an attempt to leave no stone unturned.

## Attempts to Increase Flow of Refugees from the Balkans through Yugoslavia and Turkey

With the tragic turn of events in Hungary, the Board has intensified its efforts to develop a flow of refugees in two general directions. It has, in the first place, been devoting itself to opening channels through Yugoslavia and Italy. Funds have been sent in order to facilitate the rescue operations across the Adriatic and it is hoped that some refugees in Hungary will seep through this avenue of escape. In the second place, the Board has been involved in developing plans for substantial rescue operations through Rumania and thence by sea to Turkey and Palestine. The latter plan has been the more productive. The Rumanian authorities have set up a new bureau to facilitate emigration and five small ships have been made available for rescue work from Constanza to Turkey. One of these ships has already landed in Turkey with 739 refugees including 239 orphan children. As a result of Ambassador Steinhardt's efforts, transportation across Turkey has been facilitated. The Board is making every effort to coordinate the activities of private agencies, to send increased remittances to Turkey, and to take every other possible step to maintain and increase this flow.

## Military Operations

As the situation in Hungary has become increasingly desperate, the Board has received several proposals that certain military operations might take place with the possible purpose of forestalling or hindering German extermination operations. One of these was a suggestion that the railways leading from the points of deportation to the camps be bombed. This particular suggestion was discussed with Assistant Secretary of War McCloy. After careful consideration of the matter, the War Department ruled that the suggested air operation was impracticable;

- 6 -

The Board has also received a variety of other suggestions in this category. It has been suggested that the concentration and extermination centers be bombed in order that in the resultant confusion, some of the unfortunate people might be able to escape and hide. It has also been suggested that weapons be dropped by parachute simultaneously with such bombings. Finally, it has been proposed that some parachute troops be dropped to bring about disorganization and escape of the unfortunate people.

Arrangements are under way for the examination of these proposals by the competent military authorities.

### Consideration of German-Inspired Proposals to Save the Jews of Hungary

Various large-scale and somewhat fantastic proposals are now being received through neutral countries suggesting certain concessions by the Allied Governments in return for the Germans' ceasing to kill and deport the Jews of Hungary. Most, if not all, of these propositions are of dubious reliability. Nevertheless, the policy which we are following is to avoid the outright rejection of any one of these in the hope that some valid and acceptable proposal might be received.

400. 38   JEWS
Poland—

3 Oct. 44

(also see   400. 38   Jews   )
(and        400. 38   Hungary,   )
                        Czechoslovakia.)

(see previous
letters on
bombing
railroad to
extermination
centers.)

EXECUTIVE OFFICE OF THE PRESIDENT
WAR REFUGEE BOARD
WASHINGTON 25, D. C.

OFFICE OF THE
EXECUTIVE DIRECTOR

Dear Mr. McCloy:

You will recall our conversation, some time ago concerning the various proposals placed before the Board that extermination centers in Poland be bombed. I understand that the matter is now in the hands of appropriate theatre commanders.

In this connection, there follows for such consideration as it may be worth, the substance of the pertinent portions of a cable recently received from James Mann, Assistant Executive Director of the Board, who is now in England:

"Members of the Polish Government and groups interested in rescue work report that they have reliable information from the Polish underground that in all Polish concentration camps the Germans are increasing their extermination activities.

"The War Refugee Board is urged by them again to explore with the Army the possibility of bombing the extermination chambers and German barracks at largest Polish concentration camps which, they say, are subject to precision bombing since they are sufficiently detached from the concentration camps. The aforementioned persons have promised to furnish me with recent maps which I will forward to Washington by air-mail, although I assume the Army authorities have maps of such camps."

Very truly yours,

J. W. Pehle,
Executive Director.

Mr. John J. McCloy,
Assistant Secretary of War,
War Department,
Washington, D. C.

5 October 1944

MEMORANDUM FOR MR. McCLOY:

1. To note.

2. I recommend no action be taken on this, since the matter has been fully presented several times previously. It has been our position, which we have expressed to WRB, that bombing of Polish extermination centers should be within the operational responsibility of the Russian forces.

H.A.G.

9-16-44

2315 MASSACHUSETTS AVENUE, N. W.

WASHINGTON 8, D. C.

ADAMS 8800

העברי לשחרור הועד

B 96936

HEBREW COMMITTEE OF NATIONAL LIBERATION

September 16, 1944

The Joint Chiefs of Staff
Public Health Building
19th & Constitution Avenue
Washington 25, D.C.

Gentlemen:

On the advice of the Department of State, the undersigned addressed to the War Refugee Board certain proposals
regarding the rescue of the Hebrew people of Europe. Among
these proposals was the following one:

That energetic measures be taken by the government of the United States with a view to stopping
the extermination of Hebrews in Europe by the use
of poison gases. Indeed, on various occasions the
Government of the United States, through Presidential statements, has warned Germany to refrain from
the use of poison gas against either civilian or
military populations, and has declared that if pol-
son gas should be used against the inhabitants of
any one of the United Nations, the United States
would retaliate in kind against Germany.

It has been repeatedly established that hundreds
of thousands of Hebrew people in Europe were asphyxiated through the use of poisonous gases. We
therefore request that a specific warning be issued
stating that unless the practice of using poison gas
against the Hebrew people ceases forthwith, retaliation in kind will be immediately ordered against
Germany.

We beg to stress the importance of this not
solely because it might induce Nazi Germany to stop
the use of poison gas; such a warning is important
because of the constant need to impress upon Germany
the fact that the governments of the United Nations

130

The Joint Chiefs of Staff           -2-           September 16, 1944

consider and treat the Hebrew people of Europe as human beings deserving full equality and considera- tion with other members of the United Nations.

Regarding this proposal, the Hebrew Committee of National Liberation was advised by the War Refugee Board that since the proposal is one involving military consid- erations, the Board is not prepared to comment on it.

Accordingly we submit the above proposal to the Joint Chiefs of Staff, in the hope that you will give it favorable and early consideration with a view to recom- mending that action be urgently taken in connection there- with.

I should very much like an early opportunity, for myself or another representative of this Committee, orally to discuss various aspects of our proposal, and I should appreciate your informing me when it would suit a repre- sentative of the Joint Chiefs of Staff to receive us for this purpose.

I beg to remain, Gentlemen,

Yours faithfully,

Peter H. Bergson
Chairman

PHB:1

SEP 20 1944

JCS 1072

ENCLOSURE "B"

Enclosure "B"

HEBREW COMMITTEE OF NATIONAL LIBERATION
WASHINGTON, D. C.

September 16, 1944

The Joint Chiefs of Staff
Public Health Building
19th & Constitution Avenue
Washington 25, D.C.

Gentlemen:

On the advice of the Department of State, the undersigned addressed to the War Refugee Board certain proposals regarding the rescue of the Hebrew people of Europe. Among these proposals was the following one:

That energetic measures be taken by the government of the United States with a view to stopping the extermination of Hebrews in Europe by the use of poison gases. Indeed, on various occasions the Government of the United States, through Presidential statements, has warned Germany to refrain from the use of poison gas against either civilian or military populations, and has declared that if poison gas should be used against the inhabitants of any one of the United Nations, the United States would retaliate in kind against Germany.

It has been repeatedly established that hundreds of thousands of Hebrew people in Europe were asphyxiated through the use of poisonous-gases. We therefore request that a specific warning be issued stating that unless the practice of using poison gas against the Hebrew people ceases forthwith, retaliation in kind will be immediately ordered against Germany.

B 99903

We beg to stress the importance of this not solely because it might induce Nazi Germany to stop the use of poison gas; such a warning is important because of the constant need to impress upon Germany the fact that the governments of the United Nations consider and treat the Hebrew people of Europe as human beings deserving full equality and consideration with other members of the United Nations.

Regarding this proposal, the Hebrew Committee of National Liberation was advised by the War Refugee Board that since the proposal is one involving military considerations, the Board is not prepared to comment on it.

Accordingly we submit the above proposal to the Joint Chiefs of Staff, in the hope that you will give it favorable and early consideration with a view to recommending that action be urgently taken in connection therewith.

I should very much like an early opportunity, for myself or another representative of this Committee, orally to discuss various aspects of our proposal, and I should appreciate your informing me when it would suit a representative of the Joint Chiefs of Staff to receive us for this purpose.

I beg to remain, Gentlemen,

Yours faithfully,

/s/ PETER H. BERGSON,
Chairman.

9-18-44

JCS
CRP

19 September 1944   B 96753

REGISTERED

MEMORANDUM FOR THE JOINT STRATEGIC SURVEY COMMITTEE:

Subject: Retaliation for the extermination of Hebrews in Europe by the use of poisonous gases.

Enclosure: Letter for the Joint Chiefs of Staff from the Hebrew Committee of National Liberation, dated 16 September 1944.

The enclosure is referred to the Joint Strategic Survey Committee for draft of a reply.

When the enclosure has served its purpose it is requested that it be returned.

(SIGNED)

A. J. McFARLAND,
Brigadier General, G.S.C.,
Secretary.

cms

APPENDIX TO ENCLOSURE "A"

D R A F T

REPLY TO THE HEBREW COMMITTEE OF NATIONAL LIBERATION

The Joint Chiefs of Staff have given careful consideration to the request contained in your letter of 16 September 1944 that a specific warning be issued stating that unless the practice of using poison gas against the Hebrew people ceases forthwith, retaliation in kind will be immediately ordered against Germany.

The Joint Chiefs of Staff clearly recognize and are in sympathy with the high motive which prompts your recommendation for drastic action in this matter. However, they can not support on a logical or realistic basis the proposal that the continued use of the lethal chamber by Germany as a means of executing non-combatants justifies the threat of gas warfare against that country, - for the following reasons:

a. If gas warfare is threatened, we must be prepared to carry out the threat.

b. Such action would not prevent the mass execution of defenseless civilians, since, if the Germans under this threat actually abandoned gas as means of execution, other methods could be substituted.

c. It would remove at once all restraint in the use of gas and possibly other inhumane methods of warfare with a resulting great loss of life, among non-combatants as well as military personnel.

d. The punishment, generally speaking, would not fall on those primarily responsible for the atrocities.

The Joint Chiefs of Staff are of the opinion that the vigorous Allied offensives now being so successfully consummated and the announced policy of bringing war criminals to justice will soon bring this deplorable matter to an end.

In view of the above the Joint Chiefs of Staff consider that it should not be necessary for your committee to discuss this proposal further with a representative of the Joint Chiefs of Staff.

B 99901

J.C.S. 1072

26 September 1944

Pages 1 - 5, Incl.

Regraded UNCLASSIFIED
for JCS Note
by Secretaries,
1.3 Km 57/

COPY NO. 59

B 99898

## JOINT CHIEFS OF STAFF

## RETALIATION FOR THE EXTERMINATION OF HEBREWS IN EUROPE BY THE USE OF POISONOUS GASES

Note by the Secretaries

1. A letter from the Hebrew Committee of National Liberation, dated 16 September 1944 (Enclosure "B") was referred to the Joint Strategic Survey Committee for draft of a reply.

2. The report of the Joint Strategic Survey Committee (Enclosure "A") is submitted for consideration by the Joint Chiefs of Staff.

A. J. McFARLAND,

E. D. GRAVES, JR.,

Joint Secretariat.

JCS 1072

ENCLOSURE "A"

RETALIATION FOR EXTERMINATION OF HEBREWS
IN EUROPE BY THE USE OF POISONOUS GASES

Report by the Joint Strategic Survey Committee

THE PROBLEM

1. To draft a reply from the Joint Chiefs of Staff to the letter from the Hebrew Committee of National Liberation dated 16 September 1944.

RECOMMENDATION

2. That the Joint Chiefs of Staff approve and forward to the Hebrew Committee of National Liberation the reply proposed in the Appendix.

JCS 1072                    - 1 -                    Enclosure "A"

**THE JOINT CHIEFS OF STAFF**
WASHINGTON 25, D. C.

B10?959

27 September 1944.

RESTRICTED

MEMORANDUM FOR: ADMIRAL LEAHY
GENERAL MARSHALL
ADMIRAL KING
GENERAL ARNOLD

Subject: Retaliation for the Extermination
of Hebrews in Europe by the Use
of Poisonous Gases.

Reference: J.C.S. 1072.

J.C.S. 1072 is submitted for consideration of
the recommendation of the Joint Strategic Survey
Committee in paragraph 2 on page 1.

Brief attached.
R.S.C.

McFARLAND

Approved _____

Disapproved _____

9-29-44

ADDRESS REPLY TO
COMMANDING GENERAL ARMY AIR FORCES
WASHINGTON 25, D. C.

ATTENTION:

HEADQUARTERS, ARMY AIR FORCES
WASHINGTON

E102617

29 September 1944

MEMORANDUM FOR THE SECRETARY, JOINT CHIEFS OF STAFF

SUBJECT: Retaliation for the Extermination of Hebrews in Europe
by the Use of Poisonous Gases

REFERENCE: JCS 1072

I recommend that the Joint Chiefs of Staff dispatch the Enclosure
to the Hebrew Committee of National Liberation in lieu of the answer
proposed in Appendix to Enclosure "A" of JCS 1072.

H. H. ARNOLD
General, U.S. Army
Commanding General, Army Air Forces

Encl.

DECLASSIFIED
DOD Directive 5200.9
9/27/58

OCT 3 44

10-4-44

Substitute for the APPENDIX TO ENCLOSURE "A" of JCS1072 proposed by Gen. Arnold.

REPLY TO HEBREW COMMITTEE OF NATIONAL LIBERATION

R E D R A F T

The Joint Chiefs of Staff have given careful consideration to the request contained in your letter of 16 September 1944 that a specific warning be issued stating that unless the practice of using poison gas against the Hebrew people ceases forthwith, retaliation in kind will be immediately ordered against Germany.

The Joint Chiefs of Staff clearly recognize and are in sympathy with the motive which prompts your recommendation for drastic retaliatory action against Germany for use by that country of the lethal chamber as a means of executing non-combatants.

The use of poison gas in warfare has been a subject of continuing and careful study by the Joint Chiefs of Staff over a long period of time, and certain well-defined policies have been established. The Joint Chiefs of Staff have re-examined these policies with your proposal in mind and are unable to concur in your request.

It therefore appears unnecessary for your committee to discuss this matter further with a representative of the Joint Chiefs of Staff.

140

JCS 1072

- 2 -

Appendix to Enclosure "A"

EAR:rem

B104405

COPY

AGOB-C 291.2
(16 Sep 44) -B

29 September 1944.

Dr. Stephen Samuel Wise,
40 West 68th Street,
New York, New York.

Dear Rabbi Wise:

This is in reply to your telegram of 16 September 1944, addressed to the Secretary of War, requesting that an effort be made to rescue the Jewish population of German held Europe.

As a member of the President's War Refugee Board, the Secretary of War is acutely aware of the plight of these unfortunate people and is desirous of taking all possible measures to improve their condition.

Sincerely yours,

/s/

J. A. ULIO,
Major General,
The Adjutant General.

COPY FOR: Office, Chief of Staff,
Operations Division, WDGS.

Operations Branch, AGO _____ Ext. 2053

COPY

AGOB-C-E 291.2
(17 Sep 44)

C-O-P-Y

29 September 1944

E104406

Rabbi Israel Rosenberg,
Union of Orthodox Rabbis of
United States and Canada,
132 Nassau Street,
New York, New York.

Dear Rabbi Rosenberg:

This is in reply to your telegram of 17 September 1944, addressed to the Secretary of War, in which you submit a suggestion to stop further atrocities against civilians held in Germany.

The War Department continues to do everything in its power to rescue and relieve all victims of enemy persecution in Europe. However, it is believed that no advantage will be gained by repetition of previous warnings to German leaders, as their reiteration may be construed as threats, and may react to the detriment of all prisoners, both civilian and military, in the custody of the German Government.

Sincerely yours,

/s/

J. A. ULIO,
Major General,
The Adjutant General.

EAR:prw

AGOB-C-E 291.2
(17 Sep 44)

29 September 1944.    E104407

Mr. Jacob Rosenheim,
President, Agudas Israel World Organization,
New York, New York.

Dear Mr. Rosenheim:

This is in reply to your telegram of 17 September 1944, addressed to the Secretary of War, concerning your suggestion for the protection of Jews, Poles, Czechs and other nationals in German concentration camps.

The War Department continues to do everything in its power to rescue and relieve all victims of enemy persecution in Europe. However, it is believed that no advantage will be gained by repetition of previous warnings to German leaders, as their reiteration may be construed as threats, and may react to the detriment of all prisoners, both civilian and military, in the custody of the German Government.

Sincerely yours,

/s/

J. A. ULIO,
Major General,
The Adjutant General.

3 Incl.

THE JOINT CHIEFS OF STAFF
WASHINGTON

1 October 1944

CM-IN 610292
B102514

MEMORANDUM FOR: ADMIRAL LEAHY
GENERAL MARSHALL
ADMIRAL KING

Subject: Retaliation for the Extermination of Hebrews in Europe by
the use of poisonous gases.

References: a. J.C.S. 1072.
b. Secretariat memorandum,
27 September 1944, same
subject as above.

Enclosure: Substitute for the Appendix
to Enclosure "A" of J.C.S. 1072
Proposed by General Arnold.

J.C.S. 1072 having been submitted informally,
General Arnold recommended that the enclosure be
substituted for the Appendix to Enclosure "A" on
pages 2 and 3.

Your action is requested.

W. A. M. [signature]
McFARLAND

Approved ————————

Disapproved ————————

advise heal

SUBSTITUTE FOR THE APPENDIX TO ENCLOSURE "A"
OF J.C.S. 1072 PROPOSED BY GENERAL ARNOLD and amended by

As
R E D R A F T

REPLY TO HEBREW COMMITTEE OF NATIONAL LIBERATION

The Joint Chiefs of Staff have given careful consideration

to the request contained in your letter of 16 September 1944.

that a specific warning be issued stating that unless the prac-

tice of using poison gas against the Hebrew people ceases

forthwith, retaliation in kind will be immediately ordered

against Germany.

The Joint Chiefs of Staff clearly recognize and are in

sympathy with the motive which prompts your recommendation for

drastic retaliatory action against Germany for use by that

country of the lethal chamber as a means of executing non-

combatants.

The use of poison gas in warfare has been a subject of

continuing and careful study by the Joint Chiefs of Staff over

a long period of time, and certain well-defined policies have

been established. The Joint Chiefs of Staff have re-examined

these policies with your proposal in mind and are unable to

concur in your request

It therefore appears unnecessary for your committee to

discuss this matter further with a representative of the Joint

Chiefs of Staff.

JCS 1072                    - 2 -          Appendix to Enclosure "A"

SUBSTITUTE FOR THE APPENDIX TO ENCLOSURE "A" OF J.C.S. 1072
AS PROPOSED BY GENERAL ARNOLD AND AMENDED BY ADMIRAL LEAHY

810 3049

R E D R A F T

REPLY TO HEBREW COMMITTEE OF NATIONAL LIBERATION

The Joint Chiefs of Staff have given careful consideration to the request contained in your letter of 16 September 1944 that a specific warning be issued stating that unless the practice of using poison gas against the Hebrew people ceases forthwith, retaliation in kind will be immediately ordered against Germany.

The Joint Chiefs of Staff clearly recognize and are in sympathy with the motive which prompts your recommendation for drastic retaliatory action against Germany for use by that country of the lethal chamber as a means of executing non-combatants.

The use of poison gas in warfare has been a subject of continuing and careful study by the Joint Chiefs of Staff over a long period of time, and certain well-defined policies have been established. The Joint Chiefs of Staff have re-examined these policies with your proposal in mind and are unable to ~~concur in your request~~ of the opinion that from a military point of view it is inadvisable for the forces of the United States to use poison gas at the present time.

It therefore appears unnecessary for your committee to discuss this matter further with a representative of the Joint Chiefs of Staff.

Deletions - lined out
Additions - underlined

JCS 1072                           - 2 -                    Appendix to Enclosure "A"

TOP SECRET

JCS 180th Mtg. 3. RETALIATION FOR THE EXTERMINATION OF HEBREWS IN EUROPE
10-3-44     BY THE USE OF POISONOUS GASES
(J.C.S. 1072)

ADMIRAL LEAHY said that in J.C.S. 1072 the Hebrew Committee of National Liberation requested that Germany be warned to refrain from the use of poison gas against the Hebrew people on the threat of retaliation in kind. The Joint Strategic Survey Committee had recommended a reply by the Joint Chiefs of Staff in the appendix to Enclosure "A" to J.C.S. 1072.

ADMIRAL LEAHY then drew attention to a substitute letter proposed by General Arnold in lieu of the draft letter prepared by the Joint Strategic Survey Committee.

GENERAL ARNOLD said that after further consideration he was now of the opinion that the letter from the Hebrew Committee of National Liberation should not be answered.

ADMIRAL LEAHY said that he was unable to understand why the Committee had addressed the communication to the Joint Chiefs of Staff and expressed the thought that if any reply were made, it should simply state that from a military point of view the use of gas in retaliation would be inadvisable.

GENERAL McNARNEY doubted the advisability of informing the Committee that we would not use gas in retaliation. Such information in German hands might produce adverse reactions.

In response to a suggestion by Admiral Leahy that the communication received from the Hebrew Committee of National Liberation be turned over to the State Department, the SECRETARY said that the Committee, upon the advice of the State Department, had first addressed the War Refugee Board and that this Board had replied that, as the proposal was one involving military considerations, the Board was unable to comment on it.

ADMIRAL LEAHY suggested that a reply be made by the Joint Chiefs of Staff to the Committee, advising them that from a military point of view their proposal did not come within the cognizance of the Joint Chiefs of Staff.

ADMIRAL KING, concurring in Admiral Leahy's suggestion, said that the reply to the Committee should contain a specific repetition of their proposal.

THE JOINT CHIEFS OF STAFF:-

Agreed to inform the Hebrew Committee of National Liberation that, from a military point of view, the proposal to issue a specific warning that unless the practice of using poison gas against the Hebrew people ceases forthwith, retaliation in kind will be immediately ordered against Germany, does not come within the cognizance of the Joint Chiefs of Staff.

4 October 1944

Hebrew Committee of National Liberation,
Washington, D. C.

Gentlemen:

The Joint Chiefs of Staff have given consideration to the proposal contained in your letter of 16 September 1944, that a specific warning be issued stating that unless the practice of using poison gas against the Hebrew people ceases forthwith, retaliation in kind will immediately be ordered against Germany.

The Joint Chiefs of Staff consider that, from a military point of view, the proposal set forth in your letter does not come within their cognizance.

Sincerely yours,

For the Joint Chiefs of Staff:

(SIGNED)
WILLIAM D. LEAHY,
Admiral, U.S. Navy,
Chief of Staff to the
Commander in Chief of the Army and Navy.

OCT 6

Copy to:
Admiral Leahy
Aide to COMINCH
OPD WDGS

(J.C.S. 1042)

148

OPD
JCS
2971

6107500

File: OPD 385 CWP (4 Oct 44)

Subject: Retaliation for the Extermination of Hebrews in Europe by the Use of Poisonous Gases (JCS 1072).

## MEMORANDUM FOR RECORD:

1. JCS 1072 is report of the Joint Strategic Survey Committee with respect to letter from the Hebrew Committee of National Liberation, requesting that the U.S. Government warn Germany that retaliation in kind would be made unless Germany refrains from the use of poisonous gases in the extermination of Hebrews in Europe.

2. On 4 Oct 44 the JCS replied to Hebrew Committee of National Liberation, stating that the proposal set forth in their letter is not within the cognizance of JCS. Proposed reply in JCS 1072, pages 2-3, was not used.

3. D/F forwarding copy of JCS 1072 and copy of letter of 4 Oct 44, has been prepared for information of G-2. Copy of D/F made for Theater Group's information, with copy of JCS 1072 attached.

4. Copies of JCS letter 4 Oct 44 have been made for files.

J. C. S.

pem

150

#1+2

O.P.D., G.S.

5107499

OPERATIONS DIVISION

OPD 383 CW? (4 Oct 44)

Petition for the Extermination of Hebrews in Europe
by the Use of Poisonous Gases (JCS 1072).

5 October 1944.

X C-2

MEMO FOR RECORD:

OPD Section, 5 Oct, to G-2, fwds. for information, a copy of JCS 1072, per JCS ltr., 4 Oct, 44 to Hebrew Committee of Nat. Liberation.

X Information

1. There is attached for your information copy of JCS 1072, above subject.

2. There is also inclosed copy of letter dated 4 October 1944, from the Joint Chiefs of Staff in answer to letter of 16 September 1944 from the Hebrew Committee of National Liberation (Enclosure "B" to JCS 1072, pages 4-5). Attention is invited to the fact that this letter was dispatched instead of the draft reply contained in the Appendix to Enclosure "A" of JCS 1072, pages 2-3.

J. E. HULL,
Major General,
Acting Assistant Chief of Staff.

DAN Z. ZIMMERMAN,
Colonel, G. S. C.,
Chief, Policy Section.

2 Incls:
Incl 1 - Cy No.72 of JCS 1072.
Incl 2 - Cy of ltr 4 Oct 44 from
JCS to HCNL.

Copy for Theater Group, OPD, with
Incl 1 - Cy No.73 of JCS 1072.
Incl 2 - Cy of ltr 4 Oct 44 from
JCS to HCNL.

DOCUMENTS CONCERNING JEWS IN GERMANY/EUROPE

JOINT CHIEFS OF STAFF

Proposal by Hebrew Committee of National Liberation that unless the practice of using poison gas against the Hebrew people ceases, retaliation in kind will be ordered against Germany. September 1944. JCS discussion: CCS 385.3 (9-16-44) . OPD 385 CWP (4 Oct 44)

(1)    *

OPERATIONS & PLANS DIVISION, WAR DEPARTMENT GENERAL STAFF

(3) Proposed Air Action to Impede Deparation of Hungarian and Slovak Jews. Concerns air bombardment of railroad centers to impede deportation of Jews to Poland. OPD 383.7 (Sec. II) Case 21. RG 165, 15W3, 25/24B, Box 1304

(4) Creation of War Refugee Board for Rescue and Relief of Victims of Enemy Perscutions. OPD 334.8 War Refugee Board. Sec. I. RG 165, 15W3, 26/15E, Box 903

Office ASSISTANT SECRETARY OF WAR (McCloy)

Various references to Jews including correspondence from Executive Director, War Refugee Board. See folders under ASW 400.38 Germany; 400.38 Jews;
(5) 400.38 War Refugee Board. RG 107 ASW, 12W3, 2/17C, Box 74. See folder 400.38 Jews concerning bombing of railroad centers.

CIVIL AFFAIRS DIVISION, WAR/ARMY GENERAL STAFF

)** Displaced persons, refugees, etc. CAD 383.7 15W3, 1945-10 June 46, 17/7A, boxes 210-212; June 1946-1947, 17/9E & 10A, boxes 341-349; 1948, 17/14A,
) boxes 479-481.

ABC Files WAR/ARMY GENERAL STAFF

(7) Suggestion by Emergency Director War Refugee Bd for the aerial bombing of German Concentration camps located at Auschwitz and Birkenau in Upper Silesia. 14 November 1944. ABC 383.6 (8 Nov 43) Sec. 1A

(8) Proposals of the Emergency Committee to save the Jewish people of Europe. Included is a "Summary of Statements on Behalf of United States regarding Persecution of Jews". 15 September 1943. ABC 383.7 (28 Jan. 1944)

(9) Eisenhower's warning to the Germans concerning persons in forced labor battalions and concentration camps. 20 October 1944. ABC 387 Germany (18 Dec. 43) Sec. 7B

*Item 2 duplicates item 1 (Item 2 not attached. SEE: OPD 385 CWP case 99)

**Item 6 not attached. Cited as a source for information on displaced persons, refugees, etc.

WAR DEPARTMENT
WAR DEPARTMENT GENERAL STAFF
OPERATIONS DIVISION
WASHINGTON 25, D. C.

5104404

OPD 383.7 (5 Oct 44)

5 October 1944

MEMORANDUM FOR BRIGADIER GENERAL A.J. McFARLAND, SECRETARY,
JOINT CHIEFS OF STAFF:

Subject: Retaliation for the Extermination
of Hebrews of Europe by the Use
of Poisonous Gases.

1. Reference is made to conversation between
Brigadier General Russell of the Operations Division,
W.D.G.S., and General McFarland with regard to JCS 1072.
There are attached copies of replies made to Dr. Stephen
Samuel Wise, Rabbi Israel Rosenberg representing the Union
of Orthodox Rabbis of United States and Canada, and Mr.
Jacob Rosenheim, President, Agudas Israel World Organiza-
tion with regard to retaliation for the extermination of
Hebrews in Europe by the use of poisonous gases.

2. The letter to Dr. Wise was approved by the
War Refugee Board.

THOS. T. HANDY,
Lieutenant General,
Assistant Chief of Staff.

C. L. RUSSELL,
Brigadier General,
Deputy Chief, Theater Group, OPD, G.S.

3 Incls.
1 - Ltr for Dr. Wise dtd
   29 Sep 44. (Copy)
2 - Ltr for Rabbi Rosenberg
   dtd 29 Sep 44. (Copy).
3 - Ltr for Mr. Rosenheim
   dtd 29 Sep 44. (Copy).

OCT 7 44

10-5-44

*Doc. 8*

## BASIC LICENSES

| Organization | Country | License Number | Issue Date | Expiry Date | Total Authorized up to 2/5/45 | Last Remittance Authorized |
|---|---|---|---|---|---|---|
| American Christian Committee for Refugees | Switzerland | W-2150 | 3/8/44 | 6/30/45 | $ 149,500 | 12/1/44 |
| American Jewish Joint Distribution Committee | Switzerland | W-2106 | 1/3/44 | 11/30/44 | 1,578,000 | 11/17/44 |
| | Spain | W-2155 | 3/14/44 | none | 150,000 | 5/31/44 |
| | Portugal | W-2154 | 3/14/44 | none | 25,000 | 3/14/44 |
| | Turkey | W-2208 | 6/8/44 | 12/8/44 | none | |
| American Relief for Czechoslovakia, Inc. | Great Brit. | W-2153 | 3/23/44 | 1/31/45 | 350,000 | 10/16/44 |
| American Relief for Norway, Inc. | Sweden | W-2152 | 9/15/44 | 3/15/45 | 400,000 | 9/14/44 |
| Belgian War Relief, Inc. | Switzerland | W-2231 | 6/30/44 | 12/30/44 | 115,000 | 9/22/44 |
| French Relief Fund, Inc. | Great Brit. | W-2215 | 6/22/44 | 12/22/44 | 150,000 | 6/22/44 |
| Friends of Luxembourg, Inc. | Switzerland | W-2232 | 6/30/44 | 12/30/44 | 45,000 | 11/8/44 |
| International Rescue & Relief Committee | Switzerland | W-2138 | 2/16/44 | 7/31/45 | 150,000 | 1/19/45 |
| Jewish Labor Committee | Switzerland | W-2126 | 2/8/44 | 7/1/44 | 50,000 | 2/8/44 |
| | Portugal | W-2177 | 4/12/44 | 10/12/44 | 10,000 | 4/12/44 |

| Organization | Country | License Number | Issue Date | Expiry Date | Total Authorized up to 2/5/45 | Last Remittance Authorized |
|---|---|---|---|---|---|---|
| Poale Zion Organization & Jewish Natl.Workers Alliance | Switzerland Palestine | W-2275 W-2276 | 8/24/44 8/24/44 | 2/24/45 2/24/45 | $ 18,000 33,000 | 8/24/44 8/24/44 |
| Polish War Relief, Inc. | Great Brit. | W-2258 | 8/10/44 | 2/10/45 | 400,000 | 10/13/44 |
| The Queen Wilhelmina Fund, Inc. | Switzerland | W-2229 | 6/30/44 | 6/30/45 | 215,000 | 10/21/44 |
| Self-Help of Emigres from Central Europe, Inc. | Switzerland | W-2137 | 2/16/44 | 2/28/45 | 40,000 | 8/25/44 |
| Unitarian Service Committee | Switzerland Portugal | W-2149 W-2167 | 3/3/44 3/31/44 | 2/31/45 9/31/44 | 60,000 none | 8/31/44 |
| Union of Orthodox Rabbis | Switzerland | W-2117 | 1/22/44 | 12/31/44 | 700,000 | 1/8/45 |
| Vaad Hahatzala Emergency Committee | Turkey | W-2166 | 3/29/44 | 9/29/44 | 25,000 | 3/30/44 |
| World Jewish Congress | Switzerland | W-2115 | 1/19/44 | 10/31/44 | 200,000 | 5/4/44 |

## BASIC LICENSES

| Country | Organization | License Number | Issue Date | Expiry Date | Total Authorized up to 2/5/45 | Last Remittance Authorized |
|---|---|---|---|---|---|---|
| Switzerland | American Christian Committee for Refugees | W-2150 | 3/8/44 | 6/30/45 | $ 149,500 | 12/1/44 |
| | American Jewish Joint Distribution Committee | W-2106 | 1/3/44 | 11/30/44 | 1,578,000 | 11/17/44 |
| | Belgian War Relief, Inc. | W-2231 | 6/30/44 | 12/30/44 | 115,000 | 9/22/44 |
| | Friends of Luxembourg, Inc. | W-2232 | 6/30/44 | 12/30/44 | 45,000 | 11/8/44 |
| | International Rescue & Relief Committee | W-2138 | 2/16/44 | 7/31/45 | 150,000 | 1/19/45 |
| | Jewish Labor Committee | W-2126 | 2/8/44 | 7/1/44 | 50,000 | 2/8/44 |
| | Poale Zion Organization & Jewish Natl. Workers Alliance | W-2275 | 8/24/44 | 2/24/45 | 18,000 | 8/24/44 |
| | The Queen Wilhelmina Fund, Inc. | W-2229 | 6/30/44 | 6/30/45 | 215,000 | 10/21/44 |
| | Self-Help of Emigres from Central Europe, Inc. | W-2137 | 2/16/44 | 2/28/45 | 40,000 | 8/25/44 |
| | Unitarian Service Comm. | W-2149 | 3/3/44 | 2/31/45 | 60,000 | 8/31/44 |
| | Union of Orthodox Rabbis | W-2117 | 1/22/44 | 12/31/44 | 700,000 | 1/8/45 |
| | World Jewish Congress | W-2115 | 1/19/44 | 10/31/44 | 200,000 | 5/4/44 |

| Country | Organization | License Number | Issue Date | Expiry Date | Total Authorized up to 2/5/45 | Last Remittance Authorized |
|---|---|---|---|---|---|---|
| Spain | American Jewish Joint Distribution Committee | W-2155 | 3/14/44 | none | $ 150,000 | 5/31/44 |
| Portugal | American Jewish Joint Distribution Committee | W-2154 | 3/14/44 | none | 25,000 | 3/14/44 |
| | Jewish Labor Committee | W-2177 | 4/12/44 | 10/12/44 | 10,000 | 4/12/44 |
| | Unitarian Service Comm. | W-2167 | 3/31/44 | 9/31/44 | none | |
| Turkey | American Jewish Joint Distribution Committee | W-2208 | 6/8/44 | 12/8/44 | none | 3 |
| | Vaad Hahatzala Emergency Committee | W-2166 | 3/29/44 | 9/29/44 | 25,000 | 3/30/44 |
| Great Britain | American Relief for Czechoslovakia, Inc. | W-2153 | 3/23/44 | 1/31/45 | 350,000 | 10/16/44 |
| | French Relief Fund, Inc. | W-2215 | 6/22/44 | 12/22/44 | 150,000 | 6/22/44 |
| | Polish War Relief, Inc. | W-2258 | 8/10/44 | 2/10/45 | 400,000 | 10/13/44 |
| Sweden | American Relief for Norway, Inc. | W-2152 | 9/15/44 | 3/15/45 | 400,000 | 9/14/44 |
| Palestine | Poale Zion Organization & Jewish Natl. Workers Alliance | W-2276 | 8/24/44 | 2/24/45 | 33,000 | 8/24/44 |

## AMERICAN CHRISTIAN COMMITTEE FOR REFUGEES

| Country | Date | License Number | Amount Authorized | Nature of Operations | Control of Disbursements |
|---|---|---|---|---|---|
| Switzerland | 1/26/44 | NY 599856 | $ 30,000 | Remittance of $8000 monthly for relief in Switzerland; amended 3/8/44 to permit disbursement in France of $5000 monthly for 6 months. | W-2150 |
| | 5/20/44 | NY 628532 | 25,000 | Relief in France. | W-2150 |
| | 8/28/44 | NY 644044 | 38,500 | Relief in France. | W-2150 |
| | 12/1/44 | NY 662580 | 56,000 | Relief in France. | W-2150 |

TOTAL AMOUNT AUTHORIZED UP TO 2/5/45———$ 149,500

# AMERICAN FRIENDS SERVICE COMMITTEE

| Country | Date | License Number | Amount Authorized | Nature of Operations | Control of Disbursements |
|---------|------|----------------|-------------------|----------------------|--------------------------|
| Switzerland | 6/10/44 | Ph. 14156 | $ 25,000 | Purchase within Switzerland of food parcels for distribution by IRC among displaced persons in France. | |
| | 7/10/44 | Ph. 14294 (renewal of 14156 which was not utilized) | | Amended 8/12/44 to permit utilization of $10,000 of amount remitted for purchase of FFcs for relief in France; balance for purchase of food parcels. | Francs to be purchased as prescribed by WRB representative in Switzerland. |
| Portugal | 6/9/44 | Ph. 14150 | 25,000 | Purchase in Portugal and/or Spain of food parcels to be distributed by IRC among displaced persons in France. | |
| Sweden | 5/18/44 | Ph. 14037 | 1,600 | General refugee work in Sweden. | |

TOTAL AMOUNT AUTHORIZED UP TO 2/5/45——$ 51,600

## AMERICAN JEWISH JOINT DISTRIBUTION COMMITTEE    p.1

| Country | Date | License Number | Amount Authorized | Nature of Operations | Control of Disbursements |
|---|---|---|---|---|---|
| Switzerland | 1/4/44 | NY 597695 | $ 200,000 | Rescue and relief operations in enemy territory. | W-2106 |
| | 2/10/44 | NY 606326 | 100,000 | Purchase by IRC of food and other supplies in neutral countries and Hungary and Rumania for distribution by IRC in Rumania, Croatia, Hungary and Czechoslovakia. | |
| | 2/19/44 | NY 610223 | 36,000 | Remittance of $12,000 monthly for 3 months for purchase of food parcels in Switzerland for distribution by IRC to internees in Czechoslovakia. | |
| | 3/28/44 | NY 615631 | 200,000 | Evacuations from France and Rumania. | W-2106 |
| | 5/26/44 | NY 628855 | 200,000 | Rescue and relief operations in enemy territory. | W-2106 |
| | 5/26/44 | NY 629524 | 50,000 | Rescue and relief operations in enemy territory. | W-2106 |
| | 6/13/44 | NY 631532 | 150,000 | Rescue and relief operations in enemy territory. | W-2106 |
| | 6/22/44 | NY 634794 | 180,000 | Remittance of $25,000 monthly for 6 months through Switzerland to Shanghai for relief of refugees in Shanghai; amended 10/5/44 to increase to $35,000 monthly. | |

| Country | Date | License Number | Amount Authorized | Nature of Operations | Control of Disbursements |
|---|---|---|---|---|---|
| Switzerland | 7/14/44 | NY 638933 | $1,500,000 | $1,000,000 special rescue fund; $500,000 for rescue and relief operations in Balkans. | Under direction of WRB representative in Switzerland. |
| | 8/17/44 | NY 644885 | 125,000 | Rescue and relief operations in enemy territory. | Under direction of WRB representative in Switzerland. |
| | 8/24/44 | W-2274 | 125,000 | Rescue and relief operations in enemy territory. | Under direction of WRB representative in Switzerland. |
| | 8/31/44 | NY 646460 | 150,000 | Rescue and relief operations in enemy territory. | W-2106 |
| | 9/20/44 | NY 649914 | 150,000 | Rescue and relief operations in enemy territory. | W-2106 |
| | 10/6/44 | NY 653908 | 178,000 | Rescue and relief operations in Hungary and Slovakia. | W-2106 |
| | 10/19/44 | NY 655017 | 150,000 | Rescue and relief operations in enemy territory. | W-2106 |
| | 11/1/44 | NY 658720 | 500,000 | Rescue and relief operations in enemy territory. | Under direction of WRB representative in Switzerland. |

## AMERICAN JEWISH JOINT DISTRIBUTION COMMITTEE    p.3

| Country | Date | License Number | Amount Authorized | Nature of Operations | Control of Disbursements |
|---|---|---|---|---|---|
| Switzerland | 11/17/44 | NY 660227 | $ 150,000 | Rescue and relief operations in enemy territory. | W-2106 |
| | 11/27/44 | NY 660905 | 535,000 | Remittance of $35,000 monthly for 6 months to Switzerland for transmission to Shanghai for relief of refugees in Shanghai; amended 1/3/45 to increase to $100,000 monthly for 5 months. | |
| | 12/15/44 | NY 667342 | 400,000 | Rescue and relief operations in enemy territory. | Under direction of WRB representative in Switzerland |
| | 12/29/44 | NY 669799 | 100,000 | Purchase in Switzerland of food supplies for distribution to internees in enemy territory. | |
| | 1/3/45 | NY 670349 | 900,000 | Rescue and relief operations in enemy territory. | Under direction of WRB representative in Switzerland |
| | 1/25/45 | W-2402 | 5,000,000 | Rescue and relief operations in enemy territory. | Under direction of WRB representative in Switzerland |
| | 2/3/45 | NY 676817 | 800,000 | Rescue and relief operations in enemy territory. | Under direction of WRB representative in Switzerland |

| Country | Date | License Number | Amount Authorized | Nature of Operations | Control of Disbursements |
|---------|------|----------------|-------------------|----------------------|--------------------------|
| Italy | 6/1/44 | (Through WRB) | $ 50,000 | Remittance through US Army to Yugoslav Refugee Committee in Bari for rescue of Yugoslav refugees. | |
| | 8/8/44 | NY 643226 | 30,000 | Relief operations in southern Italy. | |
| | 8/26/44 | NY 646571 | 250,000 | Relief operations in northern Italy ($200,000); southern Italy ($50,000). | |
| | 10/6/44 | NY 653909 | 10,000 | Relief of refugees in liberated Yugoslav territory formerly interned on Island of Rab. | |
| | 1/25/45 | NY 674938 | 1,000 | Payment to Yugoslav Red Cross in Bari for relief of Yugoslav Jewish evacuees in Bari and refugees in Topusko. | |
| Turkey | 7/5/44 | NY 636791 | 100,000 | Purchase in Turkey of food parcels for distribution by IRC to internees in enemy territory. | |
| | 7/20/44 | NY 639820 | 50,000 | Payment for transportation of refugees from Turkey to Palestine. | |

(No remittances effected under JDC basic license for Turkey W-2208)

| Country | Date | License Number | Amount Authorized | Nature of Operations | Control of Disbursements |
|---------|------|----------------|-------------------|----------------------|--------------------------|
| Spain | 3/14/44 | NY 613830 | 100,000 | Rescue and relief operations in enemy territory. | W-2155 |
| | 5/31/44 | NY 630207 | 50,000 | Rescue and relief operations in enemy territory. | W-2155 |

## AMERICAN JEWISH JOINT DISTRIBUTION COMMITTEE    p.5

| Country | Date | License Number | Amount Authorized | Nature of Operations | Control of Disbursements |
|---------|------|----------------|-------------------|----------------------|--------------------------|
| Portugal | 2/18/44 | NY 585125 | $ 72,000 | Remittance of $12,000 monthly for 6 months for purchase in Portugal of food parcels for distribution among internees in Holland. | |
| | 3/14/44 | NY 613831 | 25,000 | Rescue and relief operations in enemy territory. | W-2154 |
| | 4/26/44 | NY 623152 | 5,000 | Purchase in Portugal of food parcels for distribution among internees in Germany. | |
| Sweden | 6/26/44 | NY 635401 | 5,000 | Relief of Finnish refugees in Sweden. | |
| | 9/8/44 | NY 648481 | 100,000 | Rescue and relief operations in Hungary. | Under direction of WRB representative in Sweden. |
| Great Brit. | 2/21/44 | NY 608939 | 20,000 | Remittance through British Government to Vatican for relief of Jewish Community in Rome. | |
| Palestine | 9/11/44 | NY 649137 | 481,453 | Reimbursement to Jewish Agency in Jerusalem for expense of evacuating refugees from Balkans to Palestine. | |
| | 9/22/44 | NY 651533 | 159,900 | Reimbursement to Jewish Agency in Jerusalem for expense of evacuating refugees from Balkans to Palestine. | |

TOTAL AMOUNT AUTHORIZED UP TO 2/5/45---$13,388,353

## AMERICAN RELIEF FOR CZECHOSLOVAKIA, INC.

| Country | Date | License Number | Amount Authorized | Nature of Operations | Control of Disbursements |
|---------|------|----------------|-------------------|----------------------|--------------------------|
| Great Brit. | 3/23/44 | NY 616053 | $ 150,000 | Rescue and relief operations in Czechoslovakia, Poland and France. | W-2153 |
| | 10/16/44 | NY 655466 | 200,000 | Rescue and relief operations in Czechoslovakia and other enemy areas. | W-2153 |

TOTAL AMOUNT AUTHORIZED UP TO 2/5/45——$ 350,000

## AMERICAN RELIEF FOR NORWAY, INC.

| Country | Date | License Number | Amount Authorized | Nature of Operations | Control of Disbursements |
|---------|------|----------------|-------------------|----------------------|--------------------------|
| Sweden | 3/30/44 | Ch. 26238 | $ 200,000 | Rescue and relief operations in Norway and relief of refugees in Sweden. | W-2152 |
| | 6/26/44 | Ch. 27358 | 120,000 | Remittance of $10,000 monthly for 6 months for rescue and relief operations in Norway and other enemy areas; renewed 12/1/44 for additional 6 months. | Under direction of WRB representative in Sweden. |
| | 9/14/44 | Ch. 28398 | 200,000 | Rescue and relief operations in Norway and relief of refugees in Sweden. | W-2152 |

TOTAL AMOUNT AUTHORIZED UP TO 2/5/45——$ 520,000

## BELGIAN WAR RELIEF, INC.

| Country | Date | License Number | Amount Authorized | Nature of Operations | Control of Disbursements |
|---|---|---|---|---|---|
| Switzerland | 6/30/44 | NY 636252 | $ 90,000 | Rescue and relief operations in enemy territory. | W-2231 |
| | 9/22/44 | NY 651532 | 25,000 | Rescue and relief operations in enemy territory. | W-2231 |

TOTAL AMOUNT AUTHORIZED UP TO 2/5/45———$ 115,000

## BOARD OF NATIONAL MISSIONS OF THE PRESBYTERIAN CHURCH

| Country | Date | License Number | Amount Authorized | Nature of Operations | Control of Disbursements |
|---------|------|----------------|-------------------|---------------------|--------------------------|
| Sweden | 6/26/44 | NY 635400 | $ 5,000 | Rescue and relief operations in enemy territory. | Under direction of WRB representative in Sweden. |
| | 7/15/44 | NY 639127 | 10,000 | Rescue and relief operations in enemy territory. | Under direction of WRB representative in Sweden. |

TOTAL AMOUNT AUTHORIZED UP TO 2/5/45----$ 15,000

## EMERGENCY COMMITTEE TO SAVE THE JEWISH PEOPLE OF EUROPE, INC.

| Country | Date | License Number | Amount Authorized | Nature of Operations | Control of Disbursements |
|---------|------|----------------|-------------------|----------------------|--------------------------|
| Turkey | 6/28/44 | NY 635883 | $ 5,000 | Rescue and relief operations in enemy territory. | Under direction of WRB representative in Turkey. |

TOTAL AMOUNT AUTHORIZED UP TO 2/5/45----$ 5,000

## FRENCH RELIEF FUND, INC.

| Country | Date | License Number | Amount Authorized | Nature of Operations | Control of Disbursements |
|---------|------|----------------|-------------------|----------------------|--------------------------|
| Great Brit. | 6/22/44 | NY 634836 | $ 150,000 | Rescue and relief operations in enemy territory. | W-2215 |

TOTAL AMOUNT AUTHORIZED UP TO 2/5/45———$ 150,000

## FRIENDS OF LUXEMBOURG, INC.

| Country | Date | License Number | Amount Authorized | Nature of Operations | Control of Disbursements |
|---------|------|----------------|-------------------|----------------------|--------------------------|
| Switzerland | 6/30/44 | NY 636251 | $ 20,000 | Rescue and Relief operations in enemy territory. | W-2232 |
| | 11/8/44 | NY 659611 | 25,000 | Rescue and relief operations in enemy territory. | W-2232 |

TOTAL AMOUNT AUTHORIZED UP TO 2/5/45----$ 45,000

## INTERNATIONAL RESCUE AND RELIEF COMMITTEE

| Country | Date | License Number | Amount Authorized | Nature of Operations | Control of Disbursements |
|---------|------|----------------|-------------------|----------------------|--------------------------|
| Switzerland | 2/17/44 | NY 608161 | $ 60,000 | Rescue and relief operations in norther France. | W-2138 |
| | 2/19/44 | NY 608719 | 45,000 | Remittance of $7500 monthly for 6 months for relief of Spanish Republican refugees interned in southern France. | Under direction of WRB representative in Switzerland. |
| | 8/10/44 | NY 643665 (Revoked 11/24/44) | 60,000 | Rescue and relief operations in northern France. | W-2138 |
| | 8/10/44 | NY 643666 (Revoked 11/24/44) | 30,000 | Remittance of $5000 monthly for 6 months for relief of Spanish Republican refugees in southern France. | Under direction of WRB representative in Switzerland. |
| | 1/19/45 | NY 673833 | 30,000 | Rescue and relief operations in enemy territory. | W-2138 |
| Turkey | 6/29/44 | NY 633571 | 5,000 | Rescue and relief operations in enemy territory. | Under direction of WRB representative in Turkey. |
| | 8/11/44 | NY 643830 | 30,000 | Remittance of $5000 monthly for 6 months for rescue and relief operations in enemy territory. | Under direction of WRB representative in Turkey. |
| Sweden | 8/11/44 | NY 643831 | 24,000 | Remittance of $2000 monthly for 6 months for rescue and relief operations in enemy territory; amended 10/28/44 increasing to $6000 monthly. | Under direction of WRB representative in Sweden. |

TOTAL AMOUNT AUTHORIZED UP TO 2/5/45————$ 284,000

## JEWISH LABOR COMMITTEE

| Country | Date | License Number | Amount Authorized | Nature of Operations | Control of Disbursements |
|---------|------|----------------|-------------------|----------------------|--------------------------|
| Switzerland | 2/8/44 | NY 605968 | $ 50,000 | Rescue and relief operations in enemy territory. | W-2126 |
| | 5/29/44 | NY 629993 | 5,000 | Remittance through Polish Legation, Bern, to Shanghai for relief of Polish nationals in Shanghai. | |
| Portugal | 4/10/44 | NY 620319 | 10,000 | Rescue and relief operations in enemy territory. | W-2177 |

TOTAL AMOUNT AUTHORIZED UP TO 2/5/45——$ 65,000

## POALE ZION ORGANIZATION AND
## JEWISH NATIONAL WORKERS ALLIANCE

| Country | Date | License Number | Amount Authorized | Nature of Operations | Control of Disbursements |
|---------|------|----------------|-------------------|----------------------|--------------------------|
| Switzerland | 8/23/44 | NY 645945 | $ 18,000 | Rescue and relief operations in enemy territory. (NY 663074 issued 11/27/44 permitted use of balance of $6000 to provide relief and transportation to Palestine of refugees in France) | W-2275 |
| Palestine | 8/23/44 | NY 645946 | 33,000 | Rescue and relief operations in enemy territory. | W-2276 |

TOTAL AMOUNT AUTHORIZED UP TO 2/5/45——$ 51,000

## POLISH WAR RELIEF, INC.

| Country | Date | License Number | Amount Authorized | Nature of Operations | Control of Disbursements |
|---------|------|----------------|-------------------|----------------------|--------------------------|
| Sweden | 9/12/44 | Ch. 28350 | $ 25,000 | Rescue and relief operations in enemy territory. | Under direction of WRB representative in Sweden. |
| Great Brit. | 8/10/44 | Ch. 27929 | 250,000 | Rescue and relief operations in enemy territory. | W-2258 |
| | 10/13/44 | Ch. 28779 | 150,000 | Rescue and relief operations in enemy territory. | W-2258 |

TOTAL AMOUNT AUTHORIZED UP TO 2/5/45————$ 425,000

## THE QUEEN WILHELMINA FUND, INC.

| Country | Date | License Number | Amount Authorized | Nature of Operations | Control of Disbursements |
|---------|------|----------------|-------------------|---------------------|--------------------------|
| Switzerland | 7/27/44 | NY 636253 | $ 90,000 | Rescue and relief operations in enemy territory. | W-2229 |
| | 9/22/44 | NY 651530 | 25,000 | Rescue and relief operations in enemy territory. | W-2229 |
| | 10/21/44 | NY 656743 | 100,000 | Rescue and relief operations in enemy territory. | W-2229 |

TOTAL AMOUNT AUTHORIZED UP TO 2/5/45-----$ 215,000

## SELF-HELP OF EMIGRES FROM CENTRAL EUROPE, INC.

| Country | Date | License Number | Amount Authorized | Nature of Operations | Control of Disbursements |
|---------|------|----------------|-------------------|----------------------|--------------------------|
| Switzerland | 2/17/44 | NY 608160 | $ 3,000 | Rescue and relief operations in enemy territory. | W-2137 |
| | 3/2/44 | NY 611370 | 20,000 | Rescue and relief operations in enemy territory. | W-2137 |
| | 8/25/44 | NY 646438 | 17,000 | Rescue and relief operations in enemy territory. | W-2137 |

TOTAL AMOUNT AUTHORIZED UP TO 2/5/45    $ 40,000

## UNITARIAN SERVICE COMMITTEE

| Country | Date | License Number | Amount Authorized | Nature of Operations | Control of Disbursements |
|---------|------|----------------|-------------------|----------------------|--------------------------|
| Switzerland | 2/28/44 | Bos. 16846 | $ 51,000 | Relief of refugees in Switzerland; administrative expenses in Switzerland. | |
| | 3/31/44 | Bos. 16843 | 30,000 | Medical aid to refugees in France; license authorized remittances to Switzerland and/or Portugal for disbursement pursuant to W-2149 and/or W-2167, governing operations from Switzerland and Portugal respectively. | W-2149 and/or W-2167 |
| | 8/31/44 | Bos. 18150 | 30,000 | Rescue and relief operations in enemy territory, particularly Balkans, Hungary and Italy. | W-2149 |

Portugal - No remittances effected under basic license for Portugal W-2167.


TOTAL AMOUNT AUTHORIZED UP TO 2/5/45----$ 111,000

## UNION OF ORTHODOX RABBIS

| Country | Date | License Number | Amount Authorized | Nature of Operations | Control of Disbursements |
|---|---|---|---|---|---|
| Switzerland | 1/24/44 | NY 602472 | $ 100,000 | Rescue and relief operations in enemy territory. | W-2117 |
| | 3/21/44 | NY 615437 | 100,000 | Rescue and relief operations in enemy territory. | W-2117 |
| | 7/8/44 | NY 637603 | 100,000 | Rescue and relief operations in enemy territory. | W-2117 |
| | 8/23/44 | NY 645950 | 100,000 | Rescue and relief operations in enemy territory | W-2117 |
| | 11/8/44 | NY 659751 | 100,000 | Rescue and relief operations in enemy territory. | W-2117 |
| | 12/11/44 | NY 666163 | 100,000 | Rescue and relief operations in enemy territory. | W-2117 |
| | 1/8/45 | NY 671422 | 100,000 | Rescue and relief operations in enemy territory. | W-2117 |

TOTAL AMOUNT AUTHORIZED UP TO 2/5/45————$ 700,000

## VAAD HAHATZALA EMERGENCY COMMITTEE

| Country | Date | License Number | Amount Authorized | Nature of Operations | Control of Disbursements |
|---|---|---|---|---|---|
| Switzerland | 3/3/44 | W-2148 | $ 50,000 | Transfer through Switzerland to Shanghai for relief of Rabbinical group in Shanghai. | |
| | 4/10/44 | NY 619706 | 20,000 | Remittance through Polish Legation, Bern, to Shanghai for relief of Rabbinical group in Shanghai. | |
| | 5/3/44 | NY 624875 | 30,100 | Remittance through Polish Legation, Bern, to Shanghai for relief of Rabbinical group in Shanghai. | |
| | 8/29/44 | NY 646936 | 20,000 | Remittance through Polish Legation, Bern, to Shanghai for relief of Rabbinical group in Shanghai. | |
| | 9/22/44 | NY 651531 | 6,000 | Remittance through Polish Legation, Bern, to Shanghai for relief of Rabbinical group in Shanghai. | |
| | 10/16/44 | NY 655482 | 25,000 | Remittance through Polish Legation, Bern, to Shanghai for relief of Rabbinical group in Shanghai. | |
| | 11/10/44 | NY 660311 | 10,000 | Remittance through Polish Legation, Bern, to Shanghai for relief of Rabbinical group in Shanghai. | |
| | 12/19/44 | NY 667892 | 13,000 | Remittance through Polish Legation, Bern, to Shanghai for relief of Rabbinical group in Shanghai. | |
| | 1/17/45 | NY 673252 | 20,000 | Remittance through Polish Legation, Bern, to Shanghai for relief of Rabbinical group in Shanghai. | |

VAAD HAHATZALA EMERGENCY COMMITTEE     p.2

| Country | Date | License Number | Amount Authorized | Nature of Operations | Control of Disbursements |
|---|---|---|---|---|---|
| Turkey | 3/30/44 | NY 617451 | $ 25,000 | Rescue and relief operations in enemy territory. | W-2166 |
| Sweden | 6/7/44 | NY 631855 | 10,000 | Rescue and relief operations in enemy territory, particularly Baltic countries. | Under direction of WRB representative in Sweden. |
| Morocco | 3/30/44 | NY 617586 | 3,000 | Purchase in Tangier of food parcels for distribution among internees in Czechoslovakia. | |
| | 9/1/44 | NY 647643 | 5,000 | Purchase in Tangier of food parcels for distribution among internees in Czechoslovakia; amended 10/5/44 to include also Hungary. | |
| | 1/9/45 | NY 671244 | 6,000 | Purchase in Tangier of food parcels for distribution among internees in Czechoslovakia and Hungary. | |
| Russia | 10/9/44 | NY 654393 | 5,200 | Relief of Rabbinical groups in areas liberated by Russia. | |

TOTAL AMOUNT AUTHORIZED UP TO 2/5/45 ---- $ 248,300

## WORLD JEWISH CONGRESS

| Country | Date | License Number | Amount Authorized | Nature of Operations | Control of Disbursements |
|---------|------|----------------|-------------------|----------------------|--------------------------|
| Switzerland | 2/4/44 | NY | $ 25,000 | Rescue and relief operations in enemy territory. | W-2115 |
| | 4/3/44 | NY 618103 | 8,010 | Relief of Italian refugees in Switzerland. | |
| | 4/3/44 | NY 618129 | 75,000 | Rescue and relief operations in enemy territory. | W-2115 |
| | 5/1/44 | NY 624166 | 4,000 | Relief of Italian refugees in Switzerland. | |
| | 5/4/44 | NY 625189 | 100,000 | Rescue and relief operations in enemy territory. | W-2115 |
| Portugal | 5/13/44 | NY 626339 | 50,000 | Rescue and relief operations in enemy territory. | Under direction of WRB representative in Portugal. |
| Sweden | 6/26/44 | NY 635350 | 10,000 | Rescue and relief operations in Bulgaria, Hungary and Rumania. | Under direction of WRB representative in Sweden. |

TOTAL AMOUNT AUTHORIZED UP TO 2/5/45-----$ 272,000

| ORGANIZATION | COUNTRY | AMOUNT | TOTAL TO 2/5/45 |
|---|---|---|---|
| American Christian Committee for Refugees | Switzerland | $ 149,500 | $ 149,500 |
| American Friends Service Committee | Switzerland | 25,000 | |
| | Portugal | 25,000 | |
| | Sweden | 1,600 | 51,600 |
| American Jewish Joint Distribution Committee | Switzerland | 11,879,000 | |
| | Italy | 341,000 | |
| | Turkey | 150,000 | |
| | Spain | 150,000 | |
| | Portugal | 102,000 | |
| | Sweden | 105,000 | |
| | Great Britain | 20,000 | |
| | Palestine | 641,353 | 13,388,353 |
| American Relief for Czechoslovakia, Inc. | Great Britain | 350,000 | 350,000 |
| American Relief for Norway, Inc. | Sweden | 520,000 | 520,000 |
| Belgian War Relief, Inc. | Switzerland | 115,000 | 115,000 |
| Board of National Missions of the Presbyterian Church | Sweden | 15,000 | 15,000 |

| ORGANIZATION | COUNTRY | AMOUNT | TOTAL TO 2/5/45 |
|---|---|---|---|
| Emergency Committee to Save the Jewish People of Europe, Inc. | Turkey | $   5,000 | $    5,000 |
| French Relief Fund, Inc. | Great Britain | 150,000 | 150,000 |
| Friends of Luxembourg, Inc. | Switzerland | 45,000 | 45,000 |
| International Rescue and Relief Committee | Switzerland Turkey Sweden | 225,000 35,000 24,000 | 284,000 |
| Jewish Labor Committee | Switzerland Portugal | 55,000 10,000 | 65,000 |
| Poale Zion Organization and Jewish National Workers Alliance | Switzerland Palestine | 18,000 33,000 | 51,000 |
| Polish War Relief, Inc. | Sweden Great Britain | 25,000 400,000 | 425,000 |
| The Queen Wilhelmina Fund, Inc. | Switzerland | 215,000 | 215,000 |
| Self-Help of Emigres from Central Europe, Inc. | Switzerland | 40,000 | 40,000 |

| ORGANIZATION | COUNTRY | AMOUNT | TOTAL TO 2/5/45 |
|---|---|---|---|
| Unitarian Service Committee | Switzerland | $ 111,000 | $ 111,000 |
| Union of Orthodox Rabbis | Switzerland | 700,000 | 700,000 |
| Vaad Hahatzala Emergency Committee | Switzerland | 194,100 | |
| | Turkey | 25,000 | |
| | Sweden | 10,000 | |
| | Morocco | 14,000 | |
| | Russia | 5,200 | 248,300 |
| World Jewish Congress | Switzerland | 212,010 | |
| | Portugal | 50,000 | |
| | Sweden | 10,000 | 272,010 |

TOTAL AMOUNT OF ALL PRIVATE AGENCY REMITTANCES AUTHORIZED UP TO 2/5/45————$17,200,763

| COUNTRY | ORGANIZATION | AMOUNT | TOTAL TO 2/5/45 |
|---------|-------------|--------|-----------------|
| Switzerland | American Christian Committee for Refugees - - - - - - - - - - - - - - - - - | $ 149,500 | |
| | American Friends Service Committee - - | 25,000 | |
| | American Jewish Joint Distribution Committee- - - - - - - - - - - - - - - - | 11,879,000 | |
| | Belgian War Relief, Inc. - - - - - - - | 115,000 | |
| | Friends of Luxembourg, Inc.- - - - - - | 45,000 | |
| | International Rescue and Relief Committee- - - - - - - - - - - - - - - - | 225,000 | |
| | Jewish Labor Committee - - - - - - - - | 55,000 | |
| | Poale Zion Organization and Jewish National Workers Alliance- - - - - - - | 18,000 | |
| | The Queen Wilhelmina Fund, Inc.- - - - | 215,000 | |
| | Self-Help of Emigres from Central Europe - - - - - - - - - - - - - - - - | 40,000 | |
| | Unitarian Service Committee- - - - - - | 111,000 | |
| | Union of Orthodox Rabbis - - - - - - - | 700,000 | |
| | Vaad Hahatzala Emergency Committee - - | 194,100 | |
| | World Jewish Congress- - - - - - - - - | 212,010 | |
| | | | $13,983,610 |
| Portugal | American Friends Service Committee - - | 25,000 | |
| | American Jewish Joint Distribution Committee- - - - - - - - - - - - - - - - | 102,000. | |
| | Jewish Labor Committee - - - - - - - - | 10,000 | |
| | World Jewish Congress- - - - - - - - - | 50,000 | |
| | | | 187,000 |

| COUNTRY | ORGANIZATION | AMOUNT | TOTAL TO 2/5/45 |
|---------|-------------|--------|-----------------|
| Sweden | American Friends Service Committee - - $ | 1,600 | |
| | American Jewish Joint Distribution Committee- - - - - - - - - - - - - - - - - | 105,000 | |
| | American Relief for Norway, Inc. - - - | 520,000 | |
| | Board of National Missions of the Presbyterian Church- - - - - - - - - - | 15,000 | |
| | International Rescue and Relief Committee- - - - - - - - - - - - - - - | 24,000 | |
| | Polish War Relief, Inc.- - - - - - - - | 25,000 | |
| | Vaad Hahatzala Emergency Committee - - | 10,000 | |
| | World Jewish Congress- - - - - - - - - | 10,000 | |
| | | | $ 710,600 |
| Italy | American Jewish Joint Distribution Committee- - - - - - - - - - - - - - - - | 341,000 | |
| | | | 341,000 |
| Turkey | American Jewish Joint Distribution Committee- - - - - - - - - - - - - - - - | 150,000 | |
| | Emergency Committee to Save the Jewish People of Europe, Inc.- - - - - | 5,000 | |
| | International Rescue and Relief Committee- - - - - - - - - - - - - - - | 35,000 | |
| | Vaad Hahatzala Emergency Committee - - | 25,000 | |
| | | | 215,000 |

| COUNTRY | ORGANIZATION | AMOUNT | TOTAL TO 2/5/45 |
|---|---|---|---|
| Spain | American Jewish Joint Distribution Committee- - - - - - - - - - - - - - - - - | $ 150,000 | |
| | | | $ 150,000 |
| Great Britain | American Jewish Joint Distribution Committee- - - - - - - - - - - - - - - | 20,000 | |
| | American Relief for Czechoslovakia - - | 350,000 | |
| | French Relief Fund, Inc. - - - - - - - | 150,000 | |
| | Polish War Relief, Inc.- - - - - - - - | 400,000 | |
| | | | 920,000 |
| Palestine | American Jewish Joint Distribution Committee- - - - - - - - - - - - - - - | 641,353 | |
| | Poale Zion Organization and Jewish National Workers Alliance- - - - - - - | 33,000 | |
| | | | 674,353 |
| Morocco | Vaad Hahatzala Emergency Committee - - | 14,000 | |
| | | | 14,000 |
| Russia | Vaad Hahatzala Emergency Committee - - | 5,200 | |
| | | | 5,200 |

TOTAL AMOUNT OF ALL PRIVATE AGENCY REMITTANCES AUTHORIZED UP TO 2/5/45 - - - -$17,200,763

## RECAPITULATION

| | |
|---|---|
| Switzerland- - - - - - - | $13,983,610 |
| Portugal - - - - - - - - | 187,000 |
| Sweden - - - - - - - - - | 710,600 |
| Italy- - - - - - - - - - | 341,000 |
| Turkey - - - - - - - - - | 215,000 |
| Spain- - - - - - - - - - | 150,000 |
| Great Britain- - - - - - | 920,000 |
| Palestine- - - - - - - - | 674,353 |
| Morocco- - - - - - - - - | 14,000 |
| Russia - - - - - - - - - | 5,200 |
| | |
| TOTAL UP TO 2/5/45 - - - | $17,200,763 |

## LICENSES ISSUED TO WAR REFUGEE BOARD

| Country | Issue Date | License Number | Amount Authorized | Purpose |
|---|---|---|---|---|
| Sweden | 6/24/44 | W-2222 | $ 50,000 | Offset transaction involving payment by WRB to Goodyear, Akron, for account its Swedish subsidiary, representing countervalue Swedish kronor acquired by WRB in Sweden for rescue and relief operations in enemy territory. |
| Sweden | 7/27/44 | NY 639174 | 50,000 | Remittance to WRB representative in Sweden for rescue and relief operations in enemy territory, from funds held in NY for account WRB representative in Turkey. |
| Sweden | 8/17/44 | W-2270 | 41,600 | Purchase in US and shipment to Sweden of 15,000 food parcels for distribution by IRC among internees in enemy territory. |
| | | Total | $ 141,600 | |

## MISCELLANEOUS REMITTANCES
### (from other than private agency funds)

| Remittance by | Country | Issue Date | License Number | Amount Authorized | Nature of Operations |
|---|---|---|---|---|---|
| Greek Government | Switzerland | 3/4/44 | Ri. 8113 | $ 5,000 | Relief of Greek nationals interned in northern Italy. |
| Gallewski, Werner | Switzerland | 7/31/44 | NY 634668 | 100 | Cable and remittance in connection with rescue of an individual in enemy territory. |
| Mirkin, Borys I. | Sweden | 6/26/44 | NY 625386 | 3,150 | To guarantee maintenance in Sweden of a Finnish refugee. |
| | | | Total | $ 8,250 | |

- - - - - - - - - - - - - - - - - - -

American Jewish Joint Distribution Committee — License No. W-2273 issued 2/21/44 authorizing negotiations with IGC, London, for underwriting by IGC of JDC local borrowing programs for relief and rescue operations in Rumania, Hungary, France and northern Italy.

## RECAPITULATION

```
Private Agency Remittances- - - - -$17,200,763
War Refugee Board Remittances - - -    141,600
Miscellaneous Remittances - - - - -      8,250
                                     _____
Total Amount of Remittances
up to 2/5/45- - - - - - - - - - - -$17,350,613
```

R Drury 2/5/45

OFFICE OF STRATEGIC SERVICES
WASHINGTON, D.C.

CONFIDENTIAL

DISTRIBUTED    23 December 1944
COUNTRY        Hungary
SUBJECT        Weiss Family and In-laws;
               Arrest of Wealthy Jewish Families
               and Permitted Escape to Portugal

SOURCE         Z
SUB SOURCE

DATE OF INFORMATION    June 1944
PLACE OF ORIGIN        Italy

DISSEMINATION NO.      A-46789
ORIGINAL REPORT NO.    GB-2975
DATE OF REPORT         11 Dec. 1944
EVALUATION             F-3

CONFIRMATION
SUPPLEMENT
CORRECTION

NUMBER OF PAGES        2
ATTACHMENTS
THEATRE

1.  Source No. 1 is a young Hungarian Reserve Army Officer, who
escaped to Rumania at the time Rumania sought an armistice
and from there came to Italy. He is a wealthy landowner,
half-Jewish and is particularly well-informed on the Jewish
situation in Hungary.

1.  A wealthy Hungarian landowner, part Jewish, told source
No. 1 in June 1944 at Budapest, that the rich Jewish industrial families of Weiss, Kornfeld, Chorin, Mauthner
and Heinrich, some 43-47 persons in all, left together to
go to Lisbon with German Gestapo permission. According
to this landowner, who is a close friend of the above
named families, an agreement was made whereby they were
to hand over all their holdings in business and industrial enterprises. The properties of Mauthner in
Derekegyhaza, of Kornfeld in Yregszense, and 3,000,000
Swiss francs paid by Chorin, were included in this turn-
over of property. The family were detained in Vienna a
month before being allowed to proceed to Lisbon. Source
understands that the preliminary arrangements in this
deal were made at Budapest.

2.  Two Hungarian officials using as one of their informants
a German SS man, informed source No. 1 that following
the month of conferences in Vienna, the main portion of
the group were allowed to proceed to Lisbon. Three
hostages were left behind in Vienna. These were, according to source's information, Alphons Weiss, Sándor
(Alexander) Kornfeld, and János (John) Mauthner. This
retention of hostages by the Germans was to insure silence
on the part of those who went to Lisbon as to what actually
happened in the negotiations at Budapest and Vienna.

II.

1. According to reliable information from Source No. 2 the Weiss family and its inlaws described in the foregoing, were transferred from Budapest to Vienna on 19 May 1944. Although the number has been reported repeatedly as 47, an unimpeachable sub-source in Lisbon has stated that only 33 persons were in the group which reached Lisbon slightly more than a month later. This same sub-source has provided the names of all those who were in the party reaching Lisbon. They were:

   Baroness Edith Weiss
   Baron Eugene (Jenő) Weiss, his wife and
   5 children,

   Baron Moricz Kornfeld, his wife and 3 children,
   Mrs. Elsa Mauthner (née Weiss) and 3 children,
   Baroness Elizabeth Weiss and 4 children,
   'r. Ferenc Chorin, his wife (née Weiss) and
   5 children,

   Dr. George (György) Hoff (of their legal staff)
   and his father and
   mother,

   Mr. and Mrs. Fenyvesi, their young daughter, and
   Mrs. Fenyvesi's mother,
   Dr. Vilmos Billitz, General manager of one of the
   family's large plants (brother of young
   Mrs. Fenyvesi.)

2. The Lisbon sub-source lists Alphons Weiss, and a son and a daughter-in-law of Baron Kornfeld as the hostages left behind in Germany, but makes no mention of János Mauthner in this connection. Also it will be noted that the family Heinrich (Gábor) is not listed among those arriving in Lisbon. It is evident that more than three persons were retained by the Germans. The same sub-source also reports that Dr. Billitz, mentioned in his list above, "was practically spirited out of Portugal in a German plane" on 27 June, within a few hours of his arrival, and taken back to Budapest presumably "without the knowledge of the Portuguese police."

167032

CONFIDENTIAL

C.I.A 109833

OFFICE OF STRATEGIC SERVICES
WASHINGTON, D.C.

DISTRIBUTED    15 January 1945
COUNTRY        Hungary
SUBJECT        Weiss Family and German Ownership of
               Manfred Weiss Industries

SOURCE         B
SUB SOURCE     As Stated

DATE OF INFORMATION    June 1944
PLACE OF ORIGIN        Italy

DISSEMINATION NO.   A-4821
ORIGINAL REPORT NO. 03-3303
DATE OF REPORT      5 January 1945
EVALUATION          F-3

COMMANDER'S
SUPPLEMENT         GB-2975,A-43789
AGREEMENT

NUMBER OF PAGES    1
ATTACHMENTS        MEDTO
THEATRE

1. About the middle of June 1944, a number of Germans appeared at the main office of the Manfred Weiss Company and produced stock certificates with proof of legal ownership, totaling a 40% interest in the Weiss works. They insisted upon securing proper (controlling) positions on the Board of Directors and a large number of places in the management. When officials of the company and members of the Government attempted to verify the transfer of these stocks by the original owners, the Weiss-Chorin families, they were told that these individuals (about third of them) had been taken to a neutral country as part of the deal. (Comment: The neutral country was Portugal).

2. Repercussions of this deal created a crisis in the Sztojay Government. Members of the cabinet who were themselves hoping to procure fat jobs and divide the spoil were enraged and helpless. Imredy was particularly embarrassed, having just accepted the post of Minister of Coordination (without portfolio) with the job of taking over the large Weiss establishments for the nation. Allegedly Horthy himself was unaware of the deal, and later received a letter of apology from Chorin, who maintained that he and his relatives were assured of Horthy's knowledge and approval of the whole matter before they had transferred their holdings.

109833

109833

DECLASSIFIED
E.O. 11652, Sec. 3(E) and 5(D) or (E)
NND 730013
By _____ NARS, Date 11 Dec 73

CONFIDENTIAL

Testimony of KURT BECHER, taken at Nürnberg,

Germany, 27 March 1946, 1000 to 1200, by

Captain Richard A. Gutman, Mr. S. Jaari, and

Mr. Richard Sonnenfeldt, Interrogators. Also

present: Mr. Leo Katz, Interpreter, and Mr.

Charles J. Gallagher, Court Reporter.

QUESTION BY MR. SONNENFELDT TO MR. KATZ?

Q  Do you solemnly swear that you will truly and faithfully translate
my question from English to German, and the responses of the witness from
German into English to the best of your ability, so help you God?

A  I do.

QUESTIONS BY MR. SONNENFELDT TO THE WITNESS THROUGH THE INTERPRETER:

Q  Do you speak English?

A  I am sorry, but a little

Q  Will you state your full name?

A  Kurt Becher.

Q  Do you solemnly swear that the testimony you are about to give will
be the truth, the whole truth and nothing but the truth, so help you God?

A  I do.

Q  When were you born?

A  12 September 1909.

Q  Where?

A  In Hamburg.

Q  What was your last official position with the German Government?

A  I was SS Unterscharfuehrer, and Chief of Special Staff of the SS
Main Operational Office.

Q  Do you know 1st Lt. and now Captain Gutman?

A  Yes, I do.

1

Q Captain Gutman (Then 1st Lt.) has already interrogated you?

A Yes.

Q You executed an affidavit for 1st Lt. and now Captain Gutman,
giving your education and your life history, is that correct?

A Yes, that is so.

Q I will now present you with the carbon copy of the affidavit that
you executed for 1st Lt. and now Captain Gutman, which was signed and sworn
to in his presence on 2 March 1946 at Oberursel, and I will ask you if
this is the same affidavit that you signed on that day?

A Yes, it is the same.

MR. SCHNENFELDT: I ask to have the affidavit which has been identified
by the witness marked as Exhibit No. A, Kurt Becher, of today.

(Whereupon the document was so marked)

Q I will now read some portions of this affidavit to you, and discuss them with you?

A Yes.

Q The affidavit states, "I have been a member of the general SS since
August 1934."

A Yes.

Q It furthermore states, "I have been a member of the NSDAP since
May 1937."

A Yes, that is so.

Q "In the Fall of 1938 I was called for a military training course of
six weeks duration with the 1st SS Deathhead Regiment at Oranienburg."

A Yes, that is so.

Q "At the beginning of the war I was Unterscharfuehrer of the SS."

A Yes.

-2-

BECHER

Q "Since that day I was not promoted any more in the General SS."

A That is also true.

Q "On 9 September 1939, I again was called to report to the 1st Deathhead Regiment (SS Totenkopf Standarte) at Oranienburg."

A Yes.

Q "On 13th September I moved with a larger SS unit to Poland as SS man, where, however, my unit was not used."

A Yes.

Q Just what did your unit do in Poland?

A My unit was occupied about two to three weeks with the loading, and with the departure from Oranienburg, and I believe my unit was never committed. That I do not know for certain.

Q Do you mean that your unit never served at the front, or, that it had no task at all during the Polish campaign?

A By that I mean they had no tasks. At any rate they did not execute any tasks.

Q Did it not have any police functions during the Polish campaign?

A The only thing that I know is that which I have already told Captain Gutman, that in one particular town my platoon, or company at one time undertook the searching of houses for weapons because the town people had been firing on units of our army from the windows. That is the only thing I knew about that.

Q The affidavit goes on to say, "In January 1941 I became Untersturm-fuehrer; in the Fall of 1941 Obersturmfuehrer, and in March 1942 Hauptsturm-fuehrer."

A Yes.

Q Continuing, "In the beginning of 1943 I became Sturmbannfuehrer; in January 1944 Obersturmfuehrer, and in January 1945 Obersturmfuehrer of the reserve."

A  Yes.

Q  What were your duties in March 1942?

A  During the month of March I was transferred to SS Operational Main Office at Berlin. It may be that at the beginning of the month of March I was still with the troops.

Q  What were your duties there?

A  My duties at the SS Main Operational Office were Inspector of the Traffic System, for riding and driving. Besides that I had the functions of an aide of Inspector Fegelein. I was also unofficially called Fegelein's Adjutant, but it was not my official position.

Q  Where were you in January 1942?

A  In a hospital.

Q  Where?

A  I was at the SS Hospital in Berlin - Lichterfelde.

Q  When were you dismissed from the hospital?

A  In February 1942.

Q  When did you first come to the hospital?

A  In December.

Q  And why?

A  I had a skin disease (VD).

Q  Where did you go after you left the hospital?

A  After I was dismissed from the hospital I remained for some time with my later office, the Inspectorate. I do not know how long I was there, but only a little time, and then I again joined the troops. With the Inspectorate I did not remain in an official capacity, but only because I was awaiting the return of the commander of the cavalry brigade, and when he returned I rejoined the troops.

Q  You were transferred to the SS Hauptamt?

4

A Yes.

Q Besides being an expert on horses, did you know anything about cars and trucks?

A About trucks I know something insofar as I was ordnance officer of the cavalry brigade, and this cavalry brigade was not entirely made up of horse troops, but also was motorized, and I know, for instance, that in the reconnaisance unit of this cavalry brigade we had trucks.

Q Do you know a man with the *Surname of Becher*, the same as yours, the Becher who was an expert in automobiles, trucks and automotive equipment in the SS Hauptamt, or, perhaps inthe RSHA?

A Sofar as I know there was nobody in the SS Main Operational Office with that name, but I am not informedaboutthe RSHA.

Q What was your position in March 1944?

A In March 1944 Iwas still the department chief, and deputy of Amt Chief in Department six of SS Main Operational Office.

Q Who was head of the Amt Six?

A Fegelein.

Q What were your exact duties?

A As department chief my duties were mostly taking care of breeding-farms for horses, and taking care of horse depots, and general questions of personnel. As Deputy Chief of Amt Six I also was responsible, of course, for the functions of the departments in the Amt.

Q What were the functions of the entire Amt?

A Supplying of the entire Waffen SS with horses,that is, takecare of the task. Then the technical training of horsemen,that is, takecare of the entire training of people who were to work with the horses, specialists on horsemanship,and on the care of horses. Then we had inspectors for thetask of inspections.

Q  In other words, your functions, as well as the function of the chief of the Art, the SS Fuehrer, and other SS heads, were entirely technically and military, is that correct?

A  By technical tasks, do you mean training and supplying of horses, and so on.

Q  What I mean, no functions other than military, is that correct?

A  Yes, that is correct.

Q  Now when did you first meet Himmler?

A  (No answer)

Q  When did you first meet Kaltenbrunner?

A  I believe I first met Kaltenbrunner in 1944.  It may be I saw him some place before that time, but I first got in touch with Kaltenbrunner, you could say, in 1944.  I saw Himmler for the first time on 27 December 1942 when I accompanied Herman Fegelein from the front to the SS Main Operational Office because the latter had been wounded.

Q  Which one was that, Walter or Herman?

A  Herman, and Himmler shook hands with me on that occasion, I believe.

Q  Will you explain to me how it happened that you changed from a purely military position into an administration position, and a position of confidence to Himmler, which had nothing to do with matters of Waffen SS; actually these were police matters, were they not.  I am referring to your part in the evacuation in the concentration camps, and particularly to your actions in Hungary?

A  I was used by my chief, Fegelein, as I have already stated, as adjutant and actual collaborator.  In this capacity I was sent to Himmler to report to him on behalf of my chief, Fegelein, during the time of 1943, to the beginning of 1944.

Q  What was Fegelein's position at that time?

A  If I remember correctly, Fegelein was Amts Chief of the Amt Six until the end of 1943, until the summer or Autumn of 1943.  The same year he was division commander, and later he became the liaison officer from Himmler to Hitler.

Q  In other words, he took the position of General Karl Wolff, is that correct?

A  Yes.

Q  Did you ever meet General Karl Wolff?

A  Yes, in passing.

Q  Will you give me a brief description of the duties of Fegelein as liaison officer between Hitler and Himmler?

A  I can only report what I know about this connection.  It is my opinion, however, that Fegelein was the actual representative of Himmler in the Fuehrer's Headquarters, and that he had to represent the interest of Himmler of the SS right there at the spot in the Fuehrer's headquarters.  I believe, however, that his position increased in the course of time, and took in more than just this function.

Q  Now when you reported to Himmler for Fegelein, what were the matters that you reported on?

A  The thing that interested us most were reports about the condition of the cavalry division.  Along with this specific interest I also reported about training conditions, inspectorate conditions, and other interest of Amt Six, but the most important was the condition of the division.

Q  Did you have any personal contact with Himmler?

A  No, I took up personal acquaintance with Himmler, and resigned from my activity in Hungary, and, there also my initial contacts were made by way of Fegelein the first few times.

-7-

BECHER

Q How did you manage to work that little deal in Hungary, when you were really a Waffen SS man?

A Originally I believe that this activity arose from Fegelein recommending me to Himmler as a business man trained at home for this job, but later I believe the other missions that I got were because I was given things for Obergruppenfuehrer Juettner, he was Chief of the Fuehrungs Hauptamt.

Q I have before me the English translation of a second affidavit, which you executed at Oberursel on 8 March 1946, in the presence of Lieutenant and now Captain Gutman, and, I shall read parts of it to you. Do you remember having executed such an affidavit?

A Yes, I have.

Q The affidavit said under paragraph one, "Approximately between the middle of September and the middle of October, 1944, I brought about the issuing of the following order with Reichsfuehrer SS Himmler of which I received two originals, one each for SS Obergruppenfuehrers Kaltenbrunner and Pohl, and a carbon copy for myself."

A Yes.

Q What do you mean by the statement, "I brought about the issuing of the following order."?

A Because of the reports on the talks I had with Himmler about my discussions, in effect an agreement with the Joint in Switzerland. I convinced Himmler that he would have to undertake something in order to have further agreements with the Joint. That is what I mean by causing the issuing of such an order.

Q You mean you were well familiar with what was going on in the concentration camps, is that why you convinced him?

A No, I mean by that only because of my negotiations that I had with

BECHER.

-8-

the Joint, I knew from these negotiations that a large scale annihilation of human beings was going on, and had to be carried on, but I had no actual information, or inside knowledge of any of these concentration camps at that time.

Q The affidavit continues: "That effective immediately I forbid any destruction (extermination) of Jews, and on the contrary that weak and sick persons must be cared for. I hold you (meaning Kaltenbrunner and Pohl) personally responsible if this order will not be complied with strictly by subordinate echelon."

Q I added the parenthesis myself.

MR SCHNENFELD: The "extermination" in parenthesis as above shown is the translators note. The "K and Pohl" in parenthesis is the note of Becher to explain the previous "you."

A Also with the subrocinate echelon.

Q I quote the words: "Effective immediately I forbid any destruction of Jews, and on the contrary that weak and sick persons must be cared for." Is that what the order provided?

A Yes.

Q Now I am going back to the first paragraph where you say, "I brought about the issuing of the following order with Reichfuehrer SS," is that correct?

A Yes.

Q Now, five minutes ago I asked if you had any knowledge what went on in concentration camps, and you said, no, is that correct?

A Yes, that is correct. I knew at that time only unofficially through the talks we had with the Joint, that destruction of Jews were going on, but I did not know anything officially. I only heard through the specialist for Jewish affairs in Hungary, Eichman, that large scale deportations of Jews from Hungary to Auschnitz were going on, and he said

they were being used for labor there.

Q In order to be able to say,"I brought about the issuance of the

order," you must have made some concrete suggestions to him, is that

correct?

A Yes.

Q If you took the responsibility for bringing about that order, for

instance, "The weak and sick persons must be cared for," then, in other

words,you must have known that weak and sick persons were not being cared

for at the time, is that correct?

A The order in its present form was dictated by Himmler in my pre-

sence. He dictated it to his secretary,Fraulein Meinert. If you are

interested in this sentence, namely,"The weakand sick persons have to

be cared for," that was not a product of my own mind, but one of us

thought it up, and he included it in the order.

Q You mean, in other words, that you had talked with Himmler, but that

he, however, formulated the order himself?

A Icaused him to issue the order,but he formulated the wording of

the order himself. When Isay that I did not know anything about the

destruction ofthe Jews, I mean by that, only I had no official insight

what was going on in the concentration camps. Of course, through my

talks with the gentlemen from the Joint, I had heard the Jews were be-

ing exterminated,and also from conversations here and there, I gathered

that people were being killed,but I do not want you to get the impres-

sion that I am an innocent individual (like an angel from heaven), and

that I never had heard anything before that time. I merely want to go

down on record for saying I had no official knowledge ofit.

Q In other words, you had no official knowledge, however unofficially you heard rumors, or statements concerning concentration camps, but had no reason for disbelieving them, is that what you want to say?

A I mean by that that at the beginning of May 1944 I learned from the conversations I had with people from the Joint, who stated to me that people who are being deported from Hungary to Auschwitzare not committed for services of labor there, but that they are being annihilated.

Q How, on the other hand, did you believe foreigners and Jews, when they told you such things, didn't you doubt their word? What was your reason for believing those people?

A The reason I believed these people, because there had been some rumors about this thing around before, and, well, I simply believed them; and, then this belief was further strengthened when Himmler issued this order. After my talking to him, and when I showed Eichmann this order in Budapest, he said, "Well, it is true, there were some Jews killed in Auschwitz, but there were also some committed for labor service," but he said, "Because of this order now all that is left for me to do is to pack up and leave. If the Jews are not being killed any more, I can not deport any more Jews to Germany."

Q I now continue with the affidavit: "I transmitted personally to Pohl a copy made for him in his office at Berlin, and left the copy made for Kaltenbrunner in the office of his secretary in Berlin," is that correct?

A Yes, that is correct.

Q "In my opinion Kaltenbrunner and Pohl are responsible for any further killings, of Jews after this date because of the above."

A Yes, that is my opinion. This order was quite clear.

Q Under paragraph two, it goes on to say, "On occasion of my visit to the concentration camp Mauthausen, 27 April 1945, 9:00 a.m., the Commandant SS Gruppenfuehrer Ziereis informed me of the following, while

BECHER

11

obligating me to the strictest secrecy," is that correct?

A That is correct.

Q "Kaltenbrunner has directed me that at least 1000 human beings must die in Mauthausen every day."

A Ziereis said in his conversation that Kaltenbrunner had given him a directive, or he had told him either 1000 people must die every day, or that he said that a thousand people must still die every day, and I did talk about the word "still" with the interrogator at the time, and I explained that it was probably caused by the fact this order was a short term order, that it had just been recently formulated.

DR SCHMEFELDT: Now I ask to have the English translation of the affidavit of 8 March 1946, executed by Becher, marked as Becher's Exhibit B of today.

(Whereupon said document was so marked)

Q Originally you were a member of the Deathhead Regiment, were you not?

A Well, I really was not a member of the Deathhead Regiment. I was a reservist - a member of the Reserves. In 1938 I was on maneuvers, and after participating in these maneuvers I received a diploma which certified that I took part in a six weeks training course, and that I obtained a rating of sufficiency," in other words, I did not excel. This six weeks training course took place in Cranienburg, and it is my opinion the reason why I was connected with the first SS Deathhead Regiment at all is because they simply had to furnish us with some quarters suitable for SS people, and, therefore, they put us into different barracks in Cranienburg. Anyway, we were transferred after eight to ten days from Cranienburg to a maneuver grounds in Luckenwalde, and did not return to Cranienburg at all after that, and that it did not really have anything to do with this first SS Deathhead Regiment, but that it was merely

BECHER

a maneuver for the line SS.

I received my red slip, and was called to report on the 1st day of September in Hamburg. We were loaded on a train and taken to Oranienburg. We were issued our clothes, and on 13 September we left. Gentlemen, if I may say, that it would not be to my discredit even if the units name at that time had been the "1st Deathhead Regiment." After the Polish campaign we were returned to Oranienburg for eight or ten days, and we just lay around there, and I did not know what unit we belonged to; then we were transferred to Munich-Dachau, which was an activation area for the Deathhead Regiment. I did not know what unit I belonged to there, because we were in the stage of being activated. From Munich-Dachau I went to the hospital, and after my release from the hospital in February 1940, I, as already requested, was transferred to a cavalry outfit, and then I was subsequently transferred. When I returned my papers were already there, and then I was transferred to the cavalry.

Q Were the Deathhead Regiments made up of concentration camp guards?

A In my opinion, no. I believe that at that time they were only people from the General SS. What I remember of that, there was a big mix-up there, and I was put into a training course of about one-hundred to one-hundred and twenty people, and they were from all kinds of companies of the General SS.

Q Can you identify the men in this picture (Becher's Exhibit No. C)?

A This is Ziereis. (indicating)

Q Is that Sutter there (indicating on a picture)?

A That tall man on the left is Ziereis at the camp. I do not know the other man.

Q Can you identify any of the men in this picture (indicating)?

A No.

13

BECHER

Q  Do you know any one in this picture (indicating)?

A  The man on the far right is Kaltenbrunner. The man in the background was the man in the accompanying and personal staff of Himmler.

Q  The man in the background of whom only a part of the face is visible, was a member of the personal accompanying staff of Himmler.

A  He was at last Sturmbannfuehrer, and I know he was always in field headquarters. The man on the extreme left is Himmler, but I do not know anybody besides him.

MR JAARI:  I ask to have this marked as Becher's Exhibit No. D.

(Whereupon the picture was so marked)

Q  Do you recognize anybody in this picture, or the scene where it was taken?

A  I have no knowledge of anybody in this picture.

Q  Do you recognize anybody in this picture?

A  The man on the left is Himmler.

Q  Do you know anybody else?

A  No, I do not know anybody else.

MR JAARI:  I ask to have this picture marked as Becher's Exhibit No. E of today.

(Whereupon the picture was so marked)

Q  Do you recognize anybody in this picture?

A  No.

Q  Do you recognize anybody in this picture?

A  I am not sure whether or not the other man is Ziereis.

Q  Is this man Scheidler, the adjutant of Kaltenbrunner?

A  No. I know him well, and this is not he.

MR SONNENFELDT:  The picture in question is document No. 3426-PS. That is all until this afternoon at 2:00 PM.

-o-o-o-o-o-o-o-o-

APPROVED:

14

Testimony of KURT BECHER, taken at Nurnberg,

Germany, 27 March 1946, 1400 to 1700, by

Captain Richard A. Gutman, Mr. S. Jaari, and

Mr. Richard Sonnenfeldt, Interrogators. Also

present: Mr. Leo Katz, Interpreter, and Mr.

Charles J. Gallagher, Court Reporter.

QUESTIONS BY MR. JAARI TO THE WITNESS THROUGH THE INTERPRETER:

Q Now you know you are still under oath?

A Yes.

Q What happened to the copy of order you had received from Himmler with regard to the stopping of extermination of Jews in the concentration camps?

A I kept this with the files I kept on the joint matters. I had a special file in which we kept the materials on the joint actions.

Q Where are these files now?

A I believe that I had this file last in Vienna during the last days of March, or perhaps the beginning of April 1945. I do not know which one of my close co-workers had this file in his custody. It is possible my personal expert Herr Oberreich may have this, and, it is also possi- ble my Adjutant Herr Leuben may have this file with him.

Q Where are these gentlemen?

A I am sorry I can not tell you. I have not seen them since the 6th of May for the last time. I would assure they are in some interment camp.

Q When the gentlemen left Vienna, where did they go?

A They went at first to Spitz on the River Danube; certainly, Herr Lueben went there. Then also they may have gone to Krumau on the Bavarian frontier. My staff was supposed to collect again at Spitz.

-1-

BECHER

Q I would like to have the full names of Oberreich and Lueben?

A Otto Oberreich and Harry Lueben.

Q Otto Oberreich, can you give us a little more information about his identify, his age, his looks and his rank?

A He is about forty years old, rather heavy set, wears glasses. He was a S3 man in the Waffen SS.

Q In the General S3 was he a member?

A Not at all. He is an old business associate of mine, and was in my old branch at Magdeburg. I had him come over and join me, because I liked to have him work with me. He is an old acquaintance of mine.

Q In what capacity, or what field did you work?

A Originally we wanted to have him as an expert on farms, in the affair of Manfred Weiss firm. They were dealing in seeds.

Q How did he enter the picture in the Joint negotiations?

A He did not enter the picture at all in the Joint negotiations, but I did discuss the Joint affair with him, and only for information purposes.

Q And Harry Lueben?

A Harry Lueben, Hauptsturmfuehrer, age thirty-five years, slender, no glasses.

Q Was his rank in the Waffen, or in the General S3?

A No, in the Waffen SS. I believe he was also in General SS, but I am not sure. He certainly did not hold an officer rank in the General SS.

Q Did he participate in the negotiations with the Joint?

A No. I think these two gentlemen should know where the files are, because Herr Oberreich was my representative in my office in Vienna, and Harry Lueben was my adjutant for my military and personnel staff.

Q Now let's go back to March 1944. In your affidavit 2 March 1946, this morning it was marked as Becher's Exhibit A, point two, you said

-2-

BECHER

that in March 1944, you received the order from Himmler,and from Juettner and Fegelein, to gather wholesale other equipment in Hungary, is that right?

A Yes.

Q Then you further state here that Fegelein expanded this order to cover almost every field?

A Yes, in order to procure other goods also.

A Was this a written order?

A No.

Q Well, what were the circumstances?

A In March I received an order from Obergruppenfuehrer Juettner, the Chief of the SS Main Operational Office, to organize a detail for the purposes of procuring horses,and other pieces of equipment, as I have stated in my affidavit. These people had to be experts, or at least well acquainted with this field.

Q What was your channel to Juettner?

A My channel was as follows: My chief in Amt Six was Herman Fegelein, but because Fegelein at that time was active in the Fuehrer's headquarters,I had both the duty toreport directly to my own chief, and the superior chief of the SS Main Operational Office, Obergruppenfuehrer Juettner. I was subordinate to two different organizations at the same time.

Q Did I understand youright, that you were subordinate to two different organizations at the same time?

A No, I was only under the SS Main Operational Office, and I came under two superiors, one the direct chief of my Amt, and then the chief of the main office,and, because of Fegelein's absence, I had both the right and duty to report to Juettner direct. The time when I received this order to organize together a detail of horses, and other equipment, was about the same,both of Juettner telling me about it, and of Fegelein

-3-

telling me about it.

Q  So the only thing that Fegelein told you about your mission was the same that Juettner told you?

A  Yes.

Q  And where does Himmler come into this order?

A  I received the order from both Fegelein and Juettner, and got my things ready to execute this mission, and to report on or about 20 March, I do not know exactly any more whether it was Juettner or Fegelein told me to report to Fegelein in Salzburg.

Q  To Fegelein's Headquarters.

A  Yes.  I reported the 19th or 20th of March to Fegelein near Salzburg at the Castle Klessheim.  That was the castle where Hitler held his official receptions.

Q  Now, you were in Salzburg on or about the 20th of March.

A  There I was informed by Fegelein, and I also knew from Juettner, I was to leave for Hungary to execute this mission from Fegelein, and urging that I had to report to Himmler that same evening.

Q  Where was Himmler?

A  Himmler was also in Salzburg.  I received the same mission from Himmler also, telling me I was to procure horses and other equipment in Hungary, and he also told me he had intentions to activate some divisions there.

Q  Germans or Hungarians?

A  They were supposed to be German divisions.

Q  From where?

A  Sofar as I found out later, they were concerned with the racial Germans who lived in Hungary.

Q  I shall try to refresh your memory in this matter.  You said that

BECKER

213

-4-

on or about the 19th or 20th of March you arrived in Salzburg. The con-

centration camp at Mauthausen is situated nearby?

A  That is correct.

Q  Do you know that in this area a socalled special staff Eichman was

activated?

A  No. I saw Obersturmfuehrer Eichman in Budapest for the first time.

Q  Did you know about Eichman before that?

A  As I said, I saw him for the first time, and heard him for the first

time.

Q  Did you meet the Germans who were with him in Budapest?

A  I met several single ones.

Q  Does the name of Rolf Gunther mean anything to you?

A  I know that Eichmann had a representative in Berlin. I know his

name was Gunther. I did see him once in Berlin when I went to look up

Eichmann in his office, but I had no talks or connection at all with him.

Q  Did you ever meet Otto Hunsche?

A  He was a Hauptsturmfuehrer, and had his staff in Budapest.

Q  Did you meet Franz Josef Novak, Hauptsturmfuehrer in Budapest?

A  I can not remember, but it may have been, of course.

Q  Did you meet Hartenberger?

A  No.

Q  But you certainly know Hauptsturmfuehrer Dieter Wisliceny?

A  I believe he is a heavy set person, whom I saw one time between

doors at Eichmann's office, but I am not sure.

Q  I believe he has a brother, is that right?

A  I do not know.

Q  Did you meet Abromeit?

A  I don't know.

Q  And Geschke?

A   Yes. Geschke was commander of the Security Police in Hungary.

Q   And Dannecker?

A   Yes, Dannecker was also with Eichmann.

Q   And Brunner?

A   I can not remember.

Q   And Burger?

A   I also don't know him.

Q   And Krumey?

A   Yes.

Q   And Winkelmann?

A   Yes. He was my chief.

Q   Do you know Winkelmann?

A   Yes.

Q   What was his position?

A   Winkelmann was the Higher SS and Police Leader in Hungary.

Q   Were you in close cooperation with him?

A   Yes. It is as follows:  To the Higher SS and Police Chief in his area, are subordinated all the SS and police agencies, at least, in an inspector or supervisory capacity, and also in a disciplinary capacity.

Q   Where did you live in Budapest?

A   At first I lived in the Androzcy, and later in Budadescy.

Q   Were these houses subordinated to the German Embassy?

A   No. These houses belonged to the family of Manfred Weiss, originally, and I moved into this house with my office.  Originally, all told, there were three houses, and I was placed there.  I was directed to go there, both myself and my staff.

Q   What connection did you have with the higher offices in Germany, directly by radio and telephone?

A   Both by radio and telephone, and teletype, by way of the higher

6

216

SS and police channels.

Q    Kaltenbrunner at that time was also in Budapest?

A    In the first days.

Q    With what Germans that were already there?

A    With the Adjutant Sturmbannführer Werth, and besides him, Scheidler.

Q    Who was with Scheidler, was his wife along?

A    I could not tell you about that, because I had talked to Kaltenbrunner about Budapest on the first day, but I had no personal connections with Kaltenbrunner. I never dined with him, nor was I invited by him.

Q    Can you give the approximate date when Kaltenbrunner arrived in Budapest, and left?

A    Perhaps I can; Kaltenbrunner together with Horthy went to Budapest in the same train, and on the same evening that I was in Salzburg, the 19th or 20th of March, that is, leaving Salzburg for Budapest. What I am telling you is unconfirmed. I don't have sufficient direct contact with Kaltenbrunner, but I assume that he remained there with breaks, because he had an airplane, so he also may have left a few times. He may have been away once or twice. I would assume, however, that he stayed in Budapest until the 5th to the 10th of April.

Q    You said that you spoke to Kaltenbrunner a few times. About what did you speak with him?

A    Himmler had told me I should immediately report in Budapest not only to Winkelmann, but also to Veesenmeyer.

Q    And he was the German Ambassador in Budapest?

A    Yes.

Q    You were to report to Winkelmann or to Veesenmeyer?

A    Because I could not report sufficiently to Veesenmeyer, I asked Kaltenbrunner that he should speak to Veesenmeyer, so that Veesenmeyer

7

BECHER

could support me in regard to the execution of my mission.

Q Did you have such good connection with Kaltenbrunner that you could ask him directly to support you regarding the Brigade-fuehrer Veesenmeyer?

A As well as by Himmler, as by Fegelein, I was told I should get in connection with Kaltenbrunner in Budapest, if he should be there.

Q In what capacity was Kaltenbrunner in Budapest?

A That I am telling you now is again my own opinion, which is un-confirmed. Winkelmann told me that he began his activity as Higher SS and Police Leader only after the final departure of Kaltenbrunner from Budapest.

Q Did he tell you that Kaltenbrunner already exercised these func-tions up to that time?

A Not literally, but that is the implication, or sense of this con-versation. Winkelmann had told me that his responsibility for Budapest only began on the day when Kaltenbrunner finally left again.

Q If I understand you correctly, then the Higher SS and Police Leaders were subordinate to Kaltenbrunner?

A No, Kaltenbrunner had a special position. I would state, sofar as I know, that the Higher SS and Police Leader in general did not come within Kaltenbrunner's jurisdiction, but that Kaltenbrunner in this ex-ceptional case went to Hungary, because the area southeast was es-pecially well known to him because of his Austrian connections. It is absolutely abnormal that Higher SS and Police Leader who has been determined for a certain area should only start functioning if another gentleman has finished the initial work. That is my impression.

Q How was Kaltenbrunner justified to intervene over Winkelmann's head to do things on his own?

217

8

BECHER

A If I remember correctly, was by order of Himmler.

Q which caused Kaltenbrunner to go to Budapest for this purpose?

A Yes.

Q Did you by any chance ever see this order?

A No, only as one hears generally, I learned about these things. For instance, these precise instances, as I have told you in Budapest prison.

Q What relations existed between Winkelmann and Kaltenbrunner, personal relations?

A Winkelmann knew Kaltenbrunner's power, and he was constantly striving not to get on the wrong side of him. A true friendship did not exist between Winkelmann and Kaltenbrunner. Kaltenbrunner sofar as I think never did consider Winkelmann seriously. He did not respect him as a man.

Q What was the exact source of Kaltenbrunner's power?

A In one word, he was Chief of the RSHA.

Q Was he really the Chief of the RSHA?

A Yes.

Q How do you know that?

A I have never seen a written order to that effect, but everybody knew it, every child knows that; there existed an abbreviation, CDS, Chief of the Security Police.

Q Did you ever see orders signed by Kaltenbrunner as Chief of the RSHA?

A No, sofar as I remember I never saw an order signed by Kaltenbrunner in his capacity as Chief of the RSHA. I could not say that I knew Kaltenbrunner's signature.

Q Did you during your discussions with Kaltenbrunner in Budapest see Eichmann with Kaltenbrunner?

A No, but Eichmann was with Kaltenbrunner in the Hotel Astoria.

Q Do you know Eichmann's relation to Kaltenbrunner? Were they friends? Do you know anything about that?

A No, I don't think they were friends.

Q Did they have offices established in the Hotel Astoria?

A I would say my impression is that this Hotel Astoria at least was the first place where Kaltenbrunner and his subordinate staff gathered. The offices were later established in Schwabenberg, where Eichmann's staff, and also office of Security Police were established.

Q Does the name "Sonderkommando" Eichmann mean anything to you?

A That was his firm.

Q Did you discuss with Kaltenbrunner of Eichmann's activities in Budapest?

A No. At the time when I had a conversation with Kaltenbrunner in Budapest, it was perhaps altogether only ten minutes.

Q But then you met Eichmann more frequently?

A Yes.

Q In your discussions with Eichmann, did you gain the impression, or did you find out anything from what Eichmann told you, that Eichmann's activities in Budapest were subordinate to Kaltenbrunner, or, did he report to Kaltenbrunner?

A What I tell you here is only an assumption. I believe with certainty that Eichmann did report to Kaltenbrunner at the time when Kaltenbrunner was in Budapest.

Q What reasons have you for this assumption?

A He was his chief.

Q A direct chief?

A His direct chief was Gruppenfuehrer Mueller, the Chief of Amt IV.

Q Was Mueller ever in Budapest?            1C            Becher

A  I believe, no. I never heard or saw him there.

Q  Do you know him?

A  Yes, I know him. I had to report to him. I know something quite definite. Eichmann always said to our people that his only boss was Gruppenfuehrer Mueller, and he told me this personally, that orders which were given to him by Himmler, which he had to execute, of course, he discussed these orders before with Mueller.

Q  But where was Kaltenbrunner. He was the chief of Mueller?

A  I say that Eichmann, I believe, at the time Kaltenbrunner was in Budapest, certainly received his orders from Kaltenbrunner, and did make his reports to Kaltenbrunner, but these are only assumptions of mine.

Q  However, you are quite sure that Kaltenbrunner's presence in Budapest was for official reasons, he was there for official purpose?

A  Yes, certainly, of course. I don't know what you are getting at, but I can give you an interesting explanation. I remember a conversation that took place between Winkelmann and Veesenmeyer in the detention in Budapest in December 1945, or January, 1946, I heard that the two gentlemen in their trial there, at the time when they were witnesses, learned quite independently, that between Kaltenbrunner and the Ministerial President Sztojay there were discussions about the Hungarian Jewish question, but both of them did not know that earlier. It may be interesting to you.

Q  Do you know where they learned this?

A  They learned this in the official war crimestrial in Budapest. In my presence both Winkelmann and Veesenmeyer assured/one another they knew nothing about this conversation.

Q  What was Winkelmann's viewpoint as to the Jewish question in Hungary? By that I mean, that we all know that SpecialEinsatz Commander Eichmann had come to Budapest in order to include into the final solution the Hungarian Jews.

A  I have that impression, also.

Q  That is to say, what standpoint did Winkelmann take to that?

A  Winkelmann also in December or January 1945-46, when we were in the detention ——

Q  In order to effect such a final solution by Special Commander Eich-mann, it is, of course, absolutely necessary that conversations had to precede this, and as you said, they were undertaken by Kaltenbrunner.

A  I can only say what I told you here now.  About Winkelmann's point of view, I only learned during my detention in Budapest.  However, this point of view, sofar as my activity is concerned, showed that he, I would say, in all cases did support and favored it.  I don't know what point of view Kaltenbrunner took to this question.

Q  Didn't you discuss this with Kaltenbrunner at the time in Budapest?

A  No, I was not active at that time.

Q  What do you understand by the expression, "Final solution"?

A  The words "Final solution" I heard from you just now for the first time.  From my impressions which I gained in my discussions with Eichmann, I believe Iwas able to see quite clearly that the total Jewish population of Hungary was supposed to leave that country.

Q  Did you ever hear the expression of "Final solution" before?

A  No, certainly this was the first time.

Q  Did you hear the expression "complete solution."  Did you hear the expression "special treatment."?

A  "Special treatment" I did hear.

Q  In connection with the Jewish question?

A  Please excuse me if I think about this a little.  I don't believe

BECHER

that I heard it in this connection.

Q Didn't you have the impression that Eichmann liked to employ special terms, or, perhaps, not quite clear expressions, which did not clearly give his intentions?

A Eichmann was absolutely unclear. This was based, sofar as I know, on a very strong suspicion, which he bore towards everybody. He never said what he really meant.

Q Do you know Hoess?

A I don't know the name even, and I don't know the person, either.

Q Do you know Globotchnik?

A Globotchnik at one time was Higher SS and Police Leader at Lublin, and in my capacity as Ordnance Officer, or Adjutant of Fegelein, I was at one time, together with Fegelein, with Globotchnik in a conversation at a meeting regarding the construction of a remote Amt in the general government area.

Q Did you ever meet Hoettl with Eichmann in Budapest?

A No, but I know in a conversation which I had that Eichmann and Hoettl were closely acquainted.

Q In a conversation with whom?

A Eichmann told me that.

Q But Eichmann never wanted to tell you anything definite.

A Well, it was in this way. Eichmann, for instance, was in my office, and said, "Well, I am leaving for Hoettl's place."

Q Did you meet Hoettl in Budapest?

A Yes.

Q Did you know him before?

A No.

Q In what connection did you meet Hoettl?

A  I met Hoettl in two meetings, with Winkelmann once at dinner.

Q  Was Doris there, too?

A  No, I don't know her.  At one time I was also at Hoettl's office that was his residence at the same time.  I can not remember, but I believe it was a curtesy call.  I do not believe I had any official business with him, or a discussion on official business with him.

Q  Let's go back to Eichmann.  Did you ever meet Dr. Kastner with Eichmann?

A  Yes.

Q  How was the connection between Dr Kastner and Eichmann established?

A  I can not tell you that, because it already existed, when I met Dr. Kastner, and Dr. Brandt; but I believe that Kastner and Brandt met me indirectly through Eichmann.

Q  How did you get in touch with Kastner and Brandt?

A  I believe that Brandt and Kastner were introduced to me through Eichmann.

Q  That is to say, that at that time you already had something to do with the Jewish question?

A  That began at that time.

Q  I don't understand you.  Why was Eichmann supposed to get you in touch with Brandt and Kastner?

A  I will give you an explanation.  I was already in touch with the Jewish question when I met Dr. Brandt and Kastner, because I had already undertaken the transaction Manfred Weiss.  I believe that was already concluded.

Q  That transaction with Manfred Weiss took place in April or May?

A  It was concluded by contracton 17th of May.

Q  But the signing was certainly provided by long negotiations?

BECHER

14

A Yes, one month of negotiations, testimate.

Q And that was your first connection with the Jewish question?

A Yes.

Q You understand that we are here concerned with your activity in the Jewish question, when I say connection.

A Yes.

Q Did the transaction with Manfred Weiss take place in the manner in which it is described in your German affidavit, on pages 2 and 3. There is nothing to be added or detracted from your statement?

A I described my negotiations with the Jewish Economists in detail in my own notes which were handed to you a moment ago.

Q You remained in Hungary until the end, with the exception of a few trips?

A With exception of a few trips I remained until the end in Hungary. That is to say, I remained until 18th of December in Budapest, and then undertook a trip to Germany, and in this way I did not return to Budapest any more. On the 24th or 25th of December I tried to fly to Budapest, but I did not reach it any more, because it was already encircled. I then shifted my headquarters to Vienna.

Q We shall postpone all questions about the joint negotiations until I have read your notes. We only want to discuss now what has already touched upon this morning, the Mauthausen affair.

Q May I interrupt. Just some minutes ago youasked meabout Winkelmann's attitude towards the Jewish question. Winkelmann, in December and January 1945-46, told me that Himmler almost had suspended him from the activity in the Jewish question, because of a conversation which he had one or two years previously with Himmler, who told him that he would never use Winkelmann in the Jewish question. This was upon Winkelmann's request, and Himmler confirmed this to him again, when Winkelmann was appointed Higher SS and

SS and Police Leader in Hungary. It is my duty, however, to tell you also that

I know that Eichmann had to report to Winkelmann, and that I also know that

Eichmann did actually report to Winkelmann.

Q When Eichmann had to report to Winkelmann, and, as you said, be-

fore, Kaltenbrunner had taken over, so to speak, Winkelmann's functions,

although Kaltenbrunner was not the Higher SS and Police Leader of Hungary,

isn't also to be assumed that Eichmann had to report to Kaltenbrunner at

that time?

A Yes, I said that already.

Q In the affidavit of 8 March, which we discussed this morning, you

said that Ziereis talked to you about the matter of one-thousand human

lives daily.

A On 27th of April.

Q Yes, but then you told us that already on the 20th of April Ziereis

told you something about Kaltenbrunner's plans?

A Yes. Or, let us use the word "directive." Ziereis told me, "And I person-

ally discussed the measures for Mauthausen with Kaltenbrunner."

Q Did he tell you that they discussed it, or that they agreed upon

the measures?

A Discussed it, and then he gave me all the details.

Q He told you that, "We discussed the measures," and then he gave you

the details. What were these details?

A First, in order to be quite clear I should say, perhaps, I said to

Ziereis on 20th of April, that I had plenipotentiary powers to talk with

him about the measures about the concentration camp at Mauthausen. Ziereis

was very excited about this, and replied that Himmler's representative in

southern Germany was Kaltenbrunner, and that he already had received his

directives from Kaltenbrunner. I got him finally to tell me what was

16

BECHER

intended. He swore he before that to absolute secrecy. I learned what the present number of prisoners was about twenty-five to twenty-six thousand Jews, and, well over eighty-thousand other prisoners. That this number, however, was increasedaily by return of work details. He said that he had person- ally made an agreement with Kaltenbrunner that the Jews should be housed safely, and, he spoke of the fact that about sixteen-thousand were to be placed in a camp in the forest near Wels, and that this transfer had been almost completed; and that the remaining, about ten-thousand persons were supposed to be put up on Danube barges. I found out that the equipment in the camp near Wels was by no means suitable for sixteen-thousand people to be put up in an orderly fashion, because, as Ziereis said, it was still under construction. For the remaining people, he was preparing to blow up the remaining eighty thousand in subterranean work tunnels. He told me in detail that by dummy attacks, that is to say, by means of air raid signals, he was going to get those people used to it, so that he could get them to go into the subterranean chambers, eventually, without their becoming suspicious. I asked him whether this undertaking that he had revealed to me was Kaltenbrunner's explicit order, and he answered, evasively, that he still had to go to Kaltenbrunner in order to get the order of exe- cution. This is what I heard on the 20th of April, from Ziereis.

I telephoned immediately from Mauthausen to Kaltenbrunner in Linz, and tried to bluff him that I had power of attorney from Himmler. His reaction was anger. He said to me that I couldreport to Himmler about the Jews, but I should steer clear of the other inmates of Mauthausen. Nevertheless, I asked for an immediate personal interview, which he post- poned, however, to the 23rd or 24th of April. In the evening of the 20th of April I informed Winkelmann about the entire affair in Wels, and told him that I would try by all measures to prevent this intention, disregarding any personal danger. I reported to Kaltenbrunner in the night of 25th to 26th April in Salzburg in the Hotel Oesterreichischer Hof, about two or three o'clock in the morning, of my expereince in Mauthausen. I told him of my conception about this quite frankly. Besides this intended "blow-up," I also discussed the intended putting up of the ten-thousand Jews on Danube Barges, which I also considered equivalent to a destruction. I expressed my opinion to the effect that the whole thing was a striking contradiction to my own directives from Himmler. The conversation became heated. Kaltenbrunner became excited and nervous. It vexed him conspicuously that I had gained insight into the Mauthausen affair. He asked me whe- ther I knew that Himmler was infringing constantly on Hitler's orders through my actions.

I gained the impression from Kaltenbrunner he did not know about the executive details I had learned from Ziereis, but I had the impression that the agreement in principle between Kaltenbrunner and Ziereis had been concluded. That is to say, the evacuation of the Jews, and the destruction of the remaining inmates. Upon my urging him, Kaltenbrunner gave me following new directives for Mauthausen: First, that the further evacuation of Jews should stop. Secondly, that the Jews were to be cared for decently. Thirdly, that nothing should be blown up without Kaltenbrunner's personal order. Fourth, that at the approach of American troops, the camp should be surrendered. (On 29th April, Kaltenbrunner told Winkelmann that he could now tell methat I could direct that even at the approach of Russian troops the camp could be surrendered to them).

Q  Was Neubacher present at the discussion?

A  No, but I don't even know Neubacher.

Q  Who else was present?

A  In the night from the 25th to 26th, Scheidler was present.

ECKER

18

Q. Where did you go in the morning of the 26th of April?

A. On the 26th, in the afternoon – around noon, I drove away in the direction of Mauthausen, but because I only could have arrived in Lauthausen around eight or nine o'clock in the evening, I drove to Winkelmann in Malsee that evening, and informed Winkelmann about my discussion. I remained there over night, and drove away the next morning at six o'clock to Mauthausen, where I arrived at eight o'clock. On the 27th in the morning, around half past eight, I gave personally and orally to Ziereis the four points, which had been granted by Kaltenbrunner.

Q. Did you have any order in writing by Kaltenbrunner about this?

A. No.

Q. What was Ziereis reaction?

A. Ziereis reaction was bewilderment and conspicuous anger. Ziereis told me, among other things, that he already had placed eight-hundred, or one-thousand Jews on barges, whereupon I at once ordered him to bring them back to the camp. I then drove to the camp with him, as we had met in his apartment, and he wanted to show me parts of the camp.

LR JAHRL: That is all for today. As it is late, we will continue tomorrow morning.

-0-0-0-0-0-0-

APPROVED:

_(signature)_
Interrogator

_(signature)_
Interpreter

_(signature)_
Court Reporter

228

Testimony of SS Standartenfuehrer KURT BECHER,
taken at Nurnberg, Germany, 28 March 1946, 1015 -
1200 by S. Jaari. Also present: Richard Sonnenfeldt; Bert Stein, Interpreter; Piilani A. Ahuna,
Court Reporter.

BY MR. JAARI:

Q You are the same Kurt Becher who appeared before me yesterday?

A Yes.

Q And you know that you are still making your statements under
oath?

A Yes.

Q Yesterday afternoon we had arrived at the 27th of April, 1945,
and you had just met the commandant of Mauthausen in the morning?

A Yes.

Q You had just gone to the camp with him?

A Yes.

Q Would you please describe what happened when you got into the
camp?

A Ziereis suggested that I take a short look at the camp. He
showed me, among other things, a large sick barracks with rooms for
treatment and additional tube barracks which were for the especially
privileged. They made a very good impression.

Then he went with me to the sick camp in which the poor
people were and they were in an indescribable state. In my opinion
they weighed 35 to 40 kilos.

Q Just one moment. We have heard these details about the camp,
Becher. We have also heard about the conditions in the camp. As a
matter of fact, we have enough information about that. The main issue

Becher

1

for me is that you gave Kaltenbrunner's Orders to Ziereis. I now want Ziereis's reaction.

A  I went to see the barges. During the conversation Ziereis remarked that he would not quarter Jews in barges, that he would quarter non-Jews in those barges. When I saw the Jews sitting on the bottom of that barge, pressed together like sardines, I realized that they would find a miserable death there because it was hardly possible to supply them and I do not believe there was any intention to supply them. I stated my opinion to Ziereis which he ignored. I asked him not to load anybody else in the barges.

He secretly told me that he could formally execute any order and yet do what he wanted to. Under the strictest secrecy he told me that Kaltenbrunner had said to him that at least a thousand people had to die daily.

My impression was and is that Kaltenbrunner, if this was the truth, said that to him at the same time when the personal conversation between Kaltenbrunner and Ziereis took place on the subject of the aforementioned fundamental principles.

Q  This is a deduction on your part, isn't it?

A  Yes.

Q  You do not have any concrete proof?

A  No. That was my impression. That was the impression I had.

I had the definite impression that Ziereis would have carried out, with or without the final order of Kaltenbrunner, the liquidation of the inmates if I had never intervened personally.

Q   On the 25th of April when you had your discussion with Kaltenbrunner, what reason did he give for the fact that he wanted the 80,000
non-Jews exterminated?

A   So far as I can remember, he did not elaborate on that fact at
all.

Q   I believe, however, that you, in previous interrogations, have
stated that Kaltenbrunner told you "If these 80,000 non-Jews are not
exterminated we, the Germans, will have 80,000 more enemies if the camp
is liberated."

A   It is true, I did say that to Capt. Gutman in a private talk
but I also told him that I did not remember whether Kaltenbrunner said
that himself or whether that was a private conclusion of mine which I
may have stated in my conversations with Winkelmann.

(At this point Mr. Richard Sonnenfeldt entered the room.)

Q   This, then, would be the description of the happenings between
the 20th and the 27th of April?

A   Yes.

Q   From Mauthausen you went to Dachau?

A   Yes.

Q   On the 28th of April?

A   Yes.

Q   What were the orders given by Kaltenbrunner to the Commandant
of Dachau?

A   I have to give you a short explanation.  My trip to Dachau was
preceded by a telephone conversation on the 28th with Kaltenbrunner.

3                                                            Becher

232

Kaltenbrunner told me that the matter Dachau had become obsolete because of the military situation. Nevertheless, I asked him to be permitted to go there at once and I wanted his permission to surrender the camp through a Parliamentary. Kaltenbrunner agreed.

Q    What was the name of the Commandant of Dachau?

A    I don't know it exactly. It was a Lieutenant Colonel in the SS. His name started with "W".

BY MR. SONNENFELDT:

Q    What do you know about Wolke A-1 and Wolkenbrand Veni Unewel?

A    I hear that here for the first time.

BY MR. SONNENFELDT:

Q    Do you know the Gauleiter of Bavaria?

A    I have seen the Gauleiter once, when I accompanied Winkelmann to Munich. Winkelmann was to replace Freiherr von Eberstein. Nothing was said in regard to matters concerning concentration camps.

BY MR. JAARI:

Q    But you went to Dachau in your car?

A    Yes.

Q    And on the roads, on your way, didn't you see the columns which were transporting inmates from Dachau?

A    I left Munich for Dachau at about 2000 in the evening. So far as I can remember, I did not see any columns transporting inmates.

Q    Did you see the Commandant at once upon your arrival?

A    I went at once to see him and saw him for the first time.

Q    And when you told him that the camp was to be surrendered to the Americans, didn't he object?

A    He told me that the enemy was a few kilometers from Dachau and

4

Becher

he intended to leave Dachau with his forces that evening. He also intended

to leave the inmates to the camp senior.

Q And what did he tell you about the orders he had received previously

from Kaltenbrunner?

A Nothing.

Q Absolutely nothing?

A Absolutely nothing.

Q He just said he was glad to have seen you and pushed off?

A He never spoke of any orders or directives that he might have

received from Kaltenbrunner. He told me that he did not believe that the

surrender by a Parliamentary could be carried out or whether he would have

to do it himself. He asked me whether he would have to do it himself. I

answered that in the negative, whereupon he told me he would discuss this

matter with the local Commandant and asked me for a written order. I com-

posed that written order there and handed it to him.

Q And what did he tell you that Geisler had told him to do?

A Also nothing. The camp was in a great state of excitement and

SS men were dashing in and out.

Q Did you observe whether any members of the guards had disguised

themselves?

A No.

BY MR. SONNENFELDT:

Q Have you heard anything about the use of poison gas on concentration

camp inmates?

A No.

Bedner

BY MR. JAARI:

Q  Did you ever hear of the arrival of the inmates of the camp of Muhldorf and Landsberg?

A  No.

Q  In your written statement you say that there were about 26,000 inmates in Dachau?

A  Yes.

Q  Who gave you that number?

A  The Commandant of the camp.

Q  And while you were at the camp were killings still being carried out?

A  No. I arrived there and went immediately to the CP. I stayed there for about an hour and left from that CP again so that I did not see the interior of the camp.

Q  And once more, you never heard the expression "Wolke A21" and "Wolkenbrand Kann-Klausen."

A  I hear it now for the first time.

Q  And from Dachau you then went to Salzburg where you met Winkelmann?

A  Yes.

Q  In your statement, I found an expression "Kann-Klausen." What is that?

A  That's an expression invented by me which is supposed to express the following. In short, it means that Dr. Billitz and his wife and Dr. Mariassy and his wife were to remain in Hungary if we so decided and if it was agreeable to them.

Q   And that's all?

A   That's all.

Q   You also say in your written statement that you had difficult discussions with Kaltenbrunner about this point. How did Kaltenbrunner get into the picture in the Manfred Weiss negotiations?

A   Kaltenbrunner really had nothing to do with the Manfred Weiss affair. While I was at Himmler's giving him a report, the conversation came to the subject of the persons who would remain in Germany. . . . .

MR. JAARI:  In order to make it clear as to what this is referring to, the persons in question were part of the Manfred Weiss who were to remain in Germany as a guarantee for the fulfillment of the agreement between the Manfred Weiss concern and the SS.

WITNESS: Himmler told me to discuss the details with Kaltenbrunner, who, at that time, was in the house.

Q   And what was Kaltenbrunner's attitude?

A   I got the impression that Kaltenbrunner was opposed to the entire matter.

Q   Was Kaltenbrunner responsible for the treatment and the billeting of people who were kept as security or guarantee in Germany?

A   From the conversation with Himmler I had that impression. Since Kaltenbrunner lost sight of it I was able to settle the matter to the satisfaction of the persons concerned.

Q   These "Joint" negotiations — you have described them in detail in your written statement so I do not think it is necessary to go into them.

A   Yes.

Q   However, there is one point that I would like to go into in this
case, and that is, whether Kaltenbrunner and Eichmann made things difficult.
Also, their attitude in the matter.

A   I said yesterday that I could not look through Kaltenbrunner, but
I do believe that Kaltenbrunner was against my working with the Joint...

Q   You use the word "believe". Don't you have any concrete proof?

A   He has talked to me several times in a disparaging way about my
transactions.

Q   Could you give me the day or the place when he did this?

A   I cannot recall the exact dates and places, but I do remember that
on the other hand he once told me in his office in Berlin in 1944 that he
had already suggested the same measure in 1936 without any success.  He
put nothing. . no actual obstacles in my way.

Q   How could he have done anything of this kind in 1936?  Your memory
must fail you.

A   I believe it was in 1936 but I cannot guarantee that.

Q   In 1936 he was in Austria and while there he ~~would~~ not be ~~many~~ in

Anschluss.

A   That's true.  I should like to omit the year entirely.

Q   And you don't know anything else about Kaltenbrunner in regard to
the impression he was against your actions?

A   Yes.

Q   In short, he did not put any obstacles in your way, but you had
this kind of work?

A   No.

Q   You never heard that Kaltenbrunner himself had negotiations with
foreigners about their treatment or release of Jews?

8

Becher

A   Oh yes.  In our conversation during the night from 25 to 26 April 1945 Kaltenbrunner mentioned that so far as that was concerned he himself had discussed the matter with the representative of the International Red Cross.

Q.  With whom?

A   That he did not know.

Q   From other sources you did not hear about his work, did you?

A   No.

Q   You told us yesterday that you knew Hoettl?

A   Yes.

Q   Was Hoettl a good friend of Kaltenbrunner's?

A   Oh, yes.  May I give a short explanation?

Q   Yes.

A   As proof that Kaltenbrunner and Hoettl were very close to each other, I would like to state that Hoettl, in doing his work in Hungary, often negotiated with Kaltenbrunner directly, bypassing and against Winkelmann.  I also knew that there had been differences of opinion about this between Kaltenbrunner and Winkelmann which in one case even went up to Himmler.

Q   What kind of work did Hoettl perform for Kaltenbrunner?

A   I don't know anything official about that either.  I believe that he did some intelligence work.  I know that Hoettl tried to ~~gather some~~ *take a hand* ~~in the formation of governments in Hungary.~~ *in the formation of governments in Hungary.* ~~information about the government in Hungary.~~

Q   Do you know if Hoettl, on behalf of Kaltenbrunner, had any negotiations with foreign powers?

A   Do you mean with countries exclusive of Hungary?

Q  Yes.

A  I do not know anything about that.

Q  Do you know if Hoettl himself, without Kaltenbrunner's knowledge, had negotiations with foreign powers exclusive of Hungary?

A  No. The only thing I know is that during the night of 25-26 April, while I was waiting to see Kaltenbrunner, I saw Hoettl and he told me that he, at the present time, was stationed in the neighborhood of the Swiss border.

Q  What about Eichmann? What difficulties or obstacles did he put in your way?

A  That's an interesting question. Originally Eichmann established the connection between myself and the Joint, for at that time Eichmann already worked with the Joint.

Q  With whom in the Joint?

A  In my opinion with Dr. Brandt and Dr. Kastner.

Q  Who established the connection between Eichmann and the Joint?

A  That I do not know.

Q  Continue then, with the description please.

A  At first Eichmann treated the negotiations between myself and the Joint with benevolence and furthered them. But, from his manner and action and from his statements he was not willing to fulfill the obligations to the Joint so that I subsequently had a controversy with Eichmann and he tried constantly to sabotage the fulfillment. In fact, he actually tried to ~~fo~~ *prevent it*.

Q  Who backed up Eichmann?

A  Gruppenfuehrer Mueller.

Q  You have had Himmler's support, haven't you?

X   Yes.

Q   And who backed Mueller?

A   I don't know the situation of Mueller very well.  I believe from what Eichmann told me that Mueller was very independent and autocratic. On the other hand I believe that Mueller  executed Kaltenbrunner's orders. An example.  When I at one time discussed with Kaltenbrunner the method which was opposed to what had been done formerly, Kaltenbrunner told me that Mueller executed his orders.  My reason for this discussion was that Eichmann had told me that Mueller observed my work with displeasure and he suggested to me, as a friend, to have a conversation with Mueller, for it could be possible that my person was in absolute danger.  There were many ways to liquidate people.  He mentioned, as an example, my close connection with Jews.

Q   Now, you said you talked to Kaltenbrunner about this matter.  Does that mean — have I understood you correctly — that you went to Kaltenbrunner in order to secure yourself in relations with Mueller?

A   Yes.

Q   And you did that because you knew Kaltenbrunner was Mueller's superior and Mueller had to obey Kaltenbrunner's orders?

A   To the first portion of the question, yes.  So far as the second portion is concerned, Kaltenbrunner told me that.  It was obvious that I should act this way because Kaltenbrunner was the chief of the main office and Mueller was merely the chief of a department of the main office.

Q   In your dealings with RSHA, did you have the impression, or were there any indications that Himmler was the actual chief of RSHA or was it Kaltenbrunner?

239

11

Becher

A   I was of the opinion that Kaltenbrunner was in charge of the RSHA but that he carried out orders of Himmler.

(At this point Mr. Sonnenfeldt left the room.)

Q   What was the relationship between Eichmann and Kaltenbrunner?

I mean, did you ever meet both gentlemen together?

A   No. Eichmann told me that Kaltenbrunner liked him because both of them were from Linz. There was no personal connection, however, because he was connected exclusively with his boss, Mueller.

Q   Do you know that Kaltenbrunner and Eichmann knew each other so well from childhood that they used the familiar expression "du"?

A   No, I don't believe that.

Q   Why don't you believe it?

A   Eichmann would have told me that. That's certain. When I once went with Eichmann by car he told me all these things and he never mentioned that fact.

Q   When did you see Eichmann the last time?

A   On 15 April 1945 in Wustrau by Berlin.

Q   And what did Eichmann tell you about his plans?

A   Eichmann realized what his situation was. He told me that he would never fall alive into the hands of the enemy, that he had a vial of poison which he would swallow and which would kill him at once. He did not tell me that on 15 April, but he told me that during the drive.

Q   But what did he tell you on the 15th of April about his plans?

A   Nothing. He simply stated that he wanted to go in the direction of Gauleiter Hoffer's district in order to provide billets for the 200 Jews which were to be evacuated from Theresienstadt.

240

12                                                                  Becher

Q   What was Hoffer's direction?

A   In Austria.   In don't know the exact place.   He did tell me,

however, during that trip, that he could live for years in the mountains

without any one catching him.

Q   Did he mention the Tennengeb irge mountains?

A   No.

Q   Did he ever mention Oil Stone Caves?

A   No.

Q   Did he mention his wife to you?

A   No.

Q   His mistress from Linz?

A   No.   He had told me his wife and children were living in Prague.

Q   Did he brag to you about the number of Jews he had exterminated?

A   No, he did not brag, but he did state that he had liquidated a

great number of Jews.

Q   He did not use the number 5,000,000,000?

A   No.

Q   Did he tell you that before doing anything he always took care

of having documents or letters from his superiors?

A   No, but I had the impression that he had always adjusted his

actions to Mueller.

Q   You just said that he adjusted his actions to Mueller.   Didn't

he tell you about the signed orders by Kaltenbrunner?

Becher

A   No, I had the impression that he had no direct connections with Kaltenbrunner.

MR. JAARI:   Very well, let us conclude. This other gentleman will have some questions to ask you this afternoon.

APPROVED:

_____

Interrogator

_____
Interpreter

_____
Reporter

Becher